Georg Wilhelm Friedrich Hegel, Elizabeth Sanderson Haldane

The Wisdom and Religion of a German Philosophe

Georg Wilhelm Friedrich Hegel, Elizabeth Sanderson Haldane

The Wisdom and Religion of a German Philosophe

ISBN/EAN: 9783743422452

Manufactured in Europe, USA, Canada, Australia, Japa

Cover: Foto ©Thomas Meinert / pixelio.de

Manufactured and distributed by brebook publishing software (www.brebook.com)

Georg Wilhelm Friedrich Hegel, Elizabeth Sanderson Haldane

The Wisdom and Religion of a German Philosophe

THE

WISDOM AND RELIGION

OF

A GERMAN PHILOSOPHER

BEING SELECTIONS FROM THE WRITINGS OF

G. W. F. HEGEL

COLLECTED AND EDITED BY

ELIZABETH S. HALDANE

LONDON
KEGAN PAUL, TRENCH, TRÜBNER & Co., Ltd.
PATERNOSTER HOUSE, CHARING CROSS ROAD
1897

PREFACE

IN bringing before the public a collection of extracts from the writings of a philosopher noted as much for his obscurity as his depth—a philosopher respecting whom his followers themselves appear to dispute—some apology is perhaps necessary.

No one who is acquainted with the trend of modern thought will deny that Hegel's influence is not only great, but that it tends to become greater as time goes on. And this influence is not only manifested in the higher region of speculative thought, but is also evidenced in the more ordinary relations of life —in our popular religion, in our political or social relationships, and in our views respecting education and its aims. Of course, such influence has not been directly exercised: it has come down to us through many teachers, who have drunk from the original fountain-head, and who have endeavoured to work out the ideas thus derived in manifold directions. That the work done in such a way has been of inestimable value cannot for a moment be denied; and yet the fact remains, that in this working out something has been lost from the original inspiration, and that in Hegel himself we find points stated with a direct simplicity and freshness that are wanting in the writings of many of his disciples. Hence it might seem not unfitting that we should endeavour to gather together some of the more notable of his sayings regarding the various spheres of human interest.

As far as Hegel's system of Philosophy is concerned, little or no assistance can be obtained from this collection. We cannot hope to grasp his doctrine of knowledge, of absolute reality, without penetrating his depths more fully. But we may be able to determine the key-note of his system, and apply it, each in our several ways. We may recognise something of the truth of what he teaches respecting the reality of what is rational, and the rationality of that which in verity is real; and, without trying to escape from out of our skins, from the surroundings in which we are born, and which influence us as we influence them, we may try, with Hegel, to understand these surroundings as we try to understand ourselves. We may learn that, though indeed it is requisite in the affairs of everyday life to abstract, it is surely possible at the same time to remember that we *are* abstracting, and not to take what certainly is an abstraction for absolute reality. We want, as Hegel tells us, differences, variety, in our lives, because the Absolute is richer for every difference which it embraces; but we must remember that these differences are not intelligible if taken in themselves, and without reference to the whole, which, in comprehending them, explains them.

The fact is that Hegel is so helpful just because he is so living and so concrete: it is the greatest error to suppose that he dwells in a region of abstraction remote from ordinary life. His terminology may be strange to those unaccustomed to philosophic reading, but we have only to break through the husk to find how full of meaning are his *dicta*. They differ from the brilliant half-truths—the *apperçus*—of many men of genius, which have their place, no doubt, in calling to our minds a point of view overlooked, but which will not bear a closer scrutiny. Hegel's sayings live with us, and Joy and Sorrow, Comedy and Tragedy, Life and Death, all find in him their reality as complementary factors in one great universal whole.

The pity is that an arbitrary arrangement of selections such as these gives so little idea of Hegel's riches to those who make his acquaintance for the first time. The context, which does so much to explain the meaning, is wanting, and we are reminded of a stone without its setting. But, in spite of this, a good purpose may be surely served by bringing these isolated fragments before an English-speaking public. Those who have not tried to read Hegel before may be induced to turn to the original, in order to discover the full meaning of what perhaps they rather vaguely guessed at; and those who know and value him may be reminded of passages they had forgotten; or passages which they had not specially observed may be brought before their notice. Of course, a small collection such as this is not exhaustive.

Some passages which are valued by Hegel's students will be found to be omitted, and others may be inserted which they think should be excluded. This it is difficult to avoid. I have merely taken these passages which seemed to me most likely to be useful, omitting many as repetitions, or as not comprehensible without a fuller context. Where a translation exists I have given a reference to it in brackets; but in all cases I have referred to the original, and in some cases, mainly for consistency's sake, made some slight alterations in the translator's wording. The German references are quoted from the second amended edition of Hegel's works.

I am indebted for considerable assistance in my work to the kindness of Miss Frances H. Simson, M.A., Warden of the Masson Hall, in Edinburgh.

E. S. H.

CONTENTS

PART FIRST.

	PAGE		PAGE
Thought	1	Development	30
Sober Thought	7	Morality	31
History	7	Character	33
Oratory and Argument	8	The Infinite End	33
Tragedy	9	Happiness	33
The Contingent	9	Duty	34
The Actual	9	Origin of Evil	35
Childhood	10	Badness	36
Children	11	Evil	36
Humour	12	Good and Evil	37
Chance	12	Right	38
Limitations	13	Conscience	38
Action	13	Enjoyment	38
Escaping Out of One's Time	14	Language	39
The Time Spirit	14	One's Mother Tongue	40
The Power of Life	15	Culture	40
Man and his Lot	16	Erudition	41
The State	17	Classical Knowledge	42
The Conception of Law	21	Learning	42
Nature	22	Knowledge	42
Death and Life	25	True Learning	44
Death	26	Life and Education	45
Love	27	Science	46
Apparent Depth	29	Pedantry	46
Youth	29	Dress	46
True Humility	29	Luxury	47

CONTENTS.

PART SECOND.

	PAGE		PAGE
The Nature of God	48	Conversion	72
Religion	53	Salvation	72
Different Religions	59	The Death of Christ	73
Historic Religion	60	Christ	74
Religion and the World	60	Christianity	75
Mysticism	61	Historical Christianity	79
Faith	62	The Church	79
Faith and Philosophy	65	Providence	81
The Mediator	65	The Letter of the Bible	81
Atheism	66	Body and Soul	82
Scepticism	66	Immortality	82
The Heart	66	Reconciliation	83
The Spirit of the Bible	67	Worship	84
Witness of the Spirit	68	Piety—False and True	84
Spirit	69		

PART THIRD.

Music	85	Art	86
Beauty	85	Architecture	90

PART FOURTH.

Reason	91	The Absolute	125
False Reasoning	95	Truth	126
Liberty	95	Envy	129
Freedom	96	Man's Nature	129
Necessity	103	The Finite	130
Limitation	105	Knowledge	131
The Dialectic	105	The Real and Ideal	132
Idealism	105	Age and Experience	133
Philosophy	106	Progress	134
Essence	116	The Will	134
Destiny	116	The Body and Soul	135
Self Consciousness	116	Sorrow	136
The Supersensuous	117	Spiritual Beauty	136
Dogmatism	117	Passion	136
The Idea	117	Mind	137
The Notion	122	Equality	138
Logic	123	Empiricism	138
Absolute Knowledge	124		

TRANSLATIONS MADE USE OF

Philosophy of Mind. Translated by WILLIAM WALLACE, LL.D. Clarendon Press.

The Logic (known as the *Smaller Logic*, as distinguished from the *Science of Logic*). Translated by WILLIAM WALLACE, LL.D. Clarendon Press.

Philosophy of History. Translated by J. SIBREE, M.A. Bohn's Philosophical Library.

Philosophy of Right. Translated by S. W. DYDE, M.A , D.Sc. George Bell and Sons.

History of Philosophy. Translated by E. S. HALDANE and F. H. SIMSON, M.A. Kegan Paul, Trench, Trübner & Co.

Philosophy of Religion. Translated by REV. E. B. SPEIRS, D.D., and J. C. BURDON SANDERSON. Kegan Paul, Trench, Trübner & Co.

Philosophy of Fine Art (Introduction to). Translated by BERNARD BOSANQUET, M.A Kegan Paul, Trench, Trübner & Co.

THE WISDOM AND RELIGION

OF

A GERMAN PHILOSOPHER

PART FIRST.

THOUGHT.

THOUGHT is the absolute judge, before which the content must verify and attest its claims.—*Philosophy of Religion*, vol. ii. p. 353 (iii. p. 148).

In point of content, thought is only true in proportion as it sinks itself in the facts; and in point of form, it is no private or particular state or act of the subject, but rather that attitude of consciousness where the abstract self, freed from all the special limitations to which its ordinary states or qualities are liable, restricts itself to that universal action in which it is identical with all individuals.—*The Logic*, p. 44 (p. 45).

In Thought I am free, because I am not in another, but clearly am at home with myself, and the object which to me is the essential, is in unseparated unity, my Being-for-me; and my activity in the notions that I form, is an activity in myself.—*The Phenomenology of Spirit*, p. 147.

In so far as it is said that intellect, that reason, is in the objective world, that mind and nature have universal laws, in accordance with which their life and their changes are carried on, it is conceded that the categories of thought have, in an equal degree, objective value and existence.—*The Science of Logic*, vol. i. p. 34.

The atom, in fact, is itself a thought; and hence the theory which holds matter to consist of atoms is a metaphysical theory. . . . Those who are only pure physicists are the animals; they alone do not think: but man is a thinking being, and a born metaphysician. The real question is not whether we shall apply metaphysics, but whether our metaphysics are of the right kind: in other words, whether we are not, instead of the concrete, logical idea, adopting one-sided forms of thought, rigidly fixed by the understanding, and making these the basis of our theoretical as well as our practical work. —*The Logic*, p. 194 (p. 183).

It is a self-assertion which does honour to man, to recognise nothing in sentiment which is not justified in thought. This self-will is a feature of modern times, being indeed the peculiar principle of Protestantism. What was initiated by Luther as faith in feeling and the witness of the Spirit, the more mature mind strives to apprehend in the Notion. In that way it seeks to free itself in the present, and so find itself there. It is a celebrated saying, that a half philosophy leads away from God, while a true philosophy leads to God.—*Philosophy of Right*, p. 19 (p. xxix.).

Thought is essential to humanity. It is this that distinguishes us from the brutes. In sensation, cognition, and knowledge; in our instincts and volitions, as far as they are truly human, Thought is an invariable element.—*Philosophy of History*, p. 12 (p. 9).

Thought keeps apart the moments of an object which in their separation are really one. It brought about the Fall, for man ate of the tree of the knowledge of good and evil; but it also remedies these evils.—*History of Philosophy*, vol. i. p. 296 (i. p. 274).

These philosophers brought the poetic point of view down to the prosaic, and destroyed the poetic point of view which ascribes to all that is now considered to be lifeless, a life proper to itself, perhaps also sensation, and, it may be, a being after the usual order of consciousness. The loss of this point of view is not to be lamented as if unity with nature, pure faith, innocent purity, and child-like spirit went with it. Innocent and child-like it may certainly have been, but reason is just the going forth from such innocence and unity with nature. So soon as mind grasps itself, is for itself, it must for that very reason confront the "other" of itself as a negation of consciousness, *i.e.*, look on it as something devoid of mind, an unconscious and lifeless thing, and it must first come to itself through this opposition.—*History of Philosophy*, vol. i. p. 352 (i. p. 327).

The History before us is the history of Thought finding itself, and it is the case with Thought that it only finds itself in producing itself; indeed, that it only exists and is actual in finding itself. . . . In history there is set before us what is transient, what has disappeared in the night of the past and is no more. But true, necessary Thought, with which alone we have to do, is capable of no change. —*History of Philosophy*, vol. i. p. 15 (i. p. 5).

Nothing has the pliability of Thought but Thought itself.—*History of Philosophy*, vol. i. p. 252 (i. p. 232).

Our physicists just say what they have seen, how delicate and excellent are the instruments they have made, and not what they have thought.—*History of Philosophy*, vol. ii. p. 299 (ii. p. 153).

The real work of mind is wholly and solely that of bringing to consciousness what is contained within it.—*History of Philosophy*, vol. iii. p. 18 (ii. p. 389).

It is only through man's having the power of thinking that he can make the distinction between good and evil; in thought alone is there thus the source of good and evil, but the healing of the evil which is brought about by thought is also there.—*History of Philosophy*, vol. iii. p. 93 (iii. p. 9).

It is only through thought, which casts off the particular and accidental, that the principle receives this objectivity, which is independent of mere subjectivity, and in and for itself—though in such a way that the freedom of mind still remains respected. One's own spirit must bear witness to spirit that God is Spirit; the content must be true.—*History of Philosophy*, vol. iii. p. 499 (iii. p. 423).

The world of ordinary thought, in so far as it thinks, thinks merely abstractly, it thinks only what is general; it is reserved for Spirit, which comprehends things through the Notion, to recognise the particular in the general, and to see how this particular proceeds out of the Notion by its own power.—*Philosophy of Religion*, vol. ii. p. 288 (iii. p. 78).

Thought and thought alone has eyes for the essence, substance, universal power, and ultimate design of the world. And what men call the proofs of God's existence are, rightly understood, ways of describing and analysing the native course of the mind, the course of *thought* thinking the *data* of the senses. The rise of thought beyond the world of sense, its passage from the finite to the infinite, the leap into the supersensible which it takes when it snaps asunder the chain of sense, all this transition is thought and nothing but thought. Say there must be no such passage, and you say there is to be no thinking.—*The Logic*, p. 107 (p. 103).

Actuality and thought (or Idea) are often absurdly opposed. How commonly we hear people saying that, though no objection can be urged against the truth and correctness of a certain thought, there is nothing of the kind to be seen in actuality, or it cannot be actually carried out! People who use such language only prove that they have not properly apprehended the nature either of thought or of actuality. Thought in such a case is, on one hand, the synonym for a subjective conception, plan, intention, or the like, just as actuality, on the other, is made synonymous with external and sensible existence. This is all very well in common life, where great laxity is allowed in the categories and the names given to them: and it may of course happen that, *e.g.*, the plan, or so-called idea, say of a certain method of taxation, is good and advisable in the abstract, but that nothing of the sort is found in so-called actuality, or could possibly be carried out under the given conditions. But when the abstract understanding gets hold of these categories, and exaggerates the distinction they imply into a hard and fast line of contrast, when it tells us that in this actual world we must knock ideas out of our heads, it is necessary energetically to protest against these doctrines, alike in the name of science and of sound reason. For on the one hand, Ideas are not confined to our heads merely, nor is the Idea, upon the whole, so feeble as to leave the question of its actualisation or non-actualisation dependent on our will. The Idea is rather the absolutely active as well as actual. And on the other hand, actuality is not so bad and irrational as purblind or muddle-brained would-be reformers imagine. So far is actuality, as distinguished from mere appearance, and primarily presenting a unity of inward and outward, from being in contrariety with reason, that it is rather thoroughly reasonable, and everything which is not reasonable must on that very ground cease to be held actual. The same view may be traced in the usages of educated speech, which declines to give the name of real poet or real statesman to a poet or statesman who can do nothing really meritorious or reasonable.—*The Logic*, p. 282 (p. 258).

SOBER THOUGHT.

Sober thought always has the fortunate power of not resulting in hunger and desire, but of being and remaining as it is, content. Hence by this description it is shown to be a dead understanding, for it is only death which fasts and yet rests satisfied. Neither physical life nor intellectual remains content with mere abstention; as desire it presses on through hunger and through thirst towards Truth, towards Knowledge itself.—*History of Philosophy*, vol. i. p. 30 (i. p. 18).

HISTORY.

That the History of the World, with all the changing scenes which its annals present, is this process of development and the realisation of Spirit—this is the true *Theodicæa*, the justification of God in History. Only this insight can reconcile Spirit with the History of the World, viz., that what has happened and is happening every day, is not only not "without God," but is essentially His work.—*Philosophy of History*, p. 547 (p. 477).

ORATORY AND ARGUMENT.

The special quality of eloquence is to show the manifold points of view existing in a thing, and to give force to those which harmonise with what appears to me to be most useful; it thus is the art of putting forward certain points of view in the concrete case and placing others rather in the shade. . . . What is most striking in a man, or people of culture, is the art of speaking well, or of turning subjects round and considering them in many aspects.—*History of Philosophy*, vol. ii. p. 11 (i. p. 358).

If arguments are relied upon, everything can be proved by argument, and arguments for and against can be found for everything; as particular, however, they throw no light upon the universal, the Notion. . . In the worst action there exists a point of view which is essentially real; if this is brought to the front, men excuse and vindicate the action.—*History of Philosophy*, vol. ii. p. 22 (i. p. 368).

TRAGEDY.

Misfortune is only rational when it is brought about by the will of the subject, who must be absolutely justified and moral in what he does, like the power against which he wars—which must therefore not be a merely natural power, or the power of a tyrannic will. For it is only in such a case that man himself has any part in his misfortune; natural death is merely an absolute right which nature exercises over men. Hence in what is truly tragic there must be valid moral powers on both sides which come into collision.—*History of Philosophy*, vol. ii. p. 103 (i. p. 446).

THE CONTINGENT.

Particular personality, as also the externalities of dress and the like, are no longer of importance; men let themselves be guided by general custom and fashion, since it is a matter outside of and indifferent to them not to have their own will here; for we hand over the contingent to the contingent, and only follow the external rationality that consists in identity and universality.—*History of Philosophy*, vol. i. p. 220 (i. p. 201).

THE ACTUAL.

The actuality of the rational stands opposed by the popular fancy that Ideas and ideals are nothing but chimeras, and philosophy a mere system of such phantasm. It is also opposed by the very different fancy that Ideas and ideals are something far too excellent to have actuality, or something too impotent to procure it for themselves. This divorce between idea and reality is especially dear to the analytic understanding which looks upon its own abstractions, dreams though they are, as something true and real, and prides itself on the imperative "ought," which it takes especial pleasure in prescribing even on the field of politics. As if the world had waited on it to learn how it ought to be, and was not!—*The Logic,* p. 11 (p. 11).

The object of Philosophy is the Idea; and the Idea is not so impotent as merely to have a right or an obligation to exist without actually existing.—*The Logic,* p. 10 (p. 12).

CHILDHOOD.

Child-like innocence no doubt has in it something fascinating and attractive, but only because it reminds us of what the spirit must win for itself. The harmoniousness of childhood is a gift from the hand of nature: the second harmony must spring from the labour and culture of the spirit. And so the words of Christ, "Except ye *become* as little children," &c., are very far from telling us that we must always remain children.—*The Logic,* p. 56 (p. 55).

CHILDREN.

Children should have the feeling of unity with their parents; this is the first immediately moral relationship; every teacher must respect it, keep it pure, and cultivate the sense of being thus connected. .... The worst thing which can happen to children in regard to their morality and mind is that the bond which must ever be held in reverence should become loosened or even severed, thereby causing hatred, disdain, and ill-will. Whoever does this does injury to morality in its truest form.—*History of Philosophy*, vol. ii. p. 93 (i. 437).

The necessity for the education of children is found in their inherent dissatisfaction with what they are. ... The sportive method of teaching gives to children what is childish, under the idea that it is in itself valuable. It makes not only itself ridiculous, but also all that is serious. It is scorned by the children themselves.—*Philosophy of Right*, p. 232 (p. 178).

The education and instruction of a child aim at making him actually and for himself what he is at first potentially and therefore for others, viz., for his grown-up friends. The reason, which at first exists in the child only as an inner possibility, is actualised through education; and conversely, the child by these means becomes conscious that the goodness, religion, and science which he had at first looked upon as an outward authority, are his own and inward nature.— *The Logic*, p. 278 (p. 254).

HUMOUR.

It is a pitiful wit which has no substance, and does not rest on contradictions lying in the matter itself. . . . What is really comic is to show a man or thing as they disclose themselves in their extent; and if the thing is not itself its contradiction, the comic element is superficial and groundless.—*History of Philosophy*, vol. ii. p. 83 (i. p. 427).

CHANCE.

On the surface of Nature, so to speak, Chance ranges unchecked, and that contingency must simply be recognised, without the pretension sometimes erroneously ascribed to Philosophy, of seeking to find in it a could-only-be-so-and-not-otherwise. Nor is contingency less visible in the world of Mind. The will, as we have already remarked, includes contingency under the shape of option or free choice, but only as a vanishing and abrogated element. . . . . The problem of science, and especially of Philosophy, undoubtedly consists in eliciting the necessity concealed under the semblance of contingency. That, however, is far from meaning that the contingent belongs to our subjective conception alone, and must therefore be simply set aside, if we wish to get at the truth. All scientific researches which pursue this tendency exclusively, lay themselves fairly open to the charge of mere jugglery and an overstrained precisianism.—*The Logic*, p. 290 (p. 265).

LIMITATIONS.

Man, if he wishes to be actual, must be-there-and-then, and to this end he must set a limit to himself. People who are too fastidious towards the finite never reach actuality, but linger lost in abstraction, and their light dies away.—*The Logic*, p. 182 (p. 173).

ACTION.

The true Being of man is really his action; in it individuality is actual, and it is this which abrogates what is merely contemplated in both its sides. We certainly find what is thought actualised in an unmoving bodily existence; but individuality asserts itself in action as a negative reality, which only is, so far as it abrogates existence.—*The Phenomenology of Spirit*, p. 234.

It is thus the actions and impulses of the individual which are an end in themselves; it is the use of capacities, the play of their manifestation, which gives life to what was formerly a dead implicitude; the implicitude is not an undeveloped, dead, and abstract universal, since it is itself immediately this present and actual in the process of individuality.—*The Phenomenology of Spirit*, p. 284.

Action changes nothing and opposes nothing. It is the pure form of translating what is invisible into the visible, and the content which is brought to light and set forth is none other than what this action already is implicitly.—*The Phenomenology of Spirit*, p. 286.

ESCAPING OUT OF ONE'S TIME.

The individual is the offspring of his people, of his world, whose constitution and attributes are alone manifested in his form; he may spread himself out as he will, he cannot escape out of his time any more than out of his skin.—*History of Philosophy*, vol. i. p. 59 (i. p. 45).

Each unit is the Son of his nation, and at the same time—in as far as the state to which he belongs is undergoing development—the Son of his Age. None remains behind it, still less advances beyond it. This Spiritual Being (the Spirit of his Time) is his; he is a representative of it; it is that in which he originated and in which he lives.—*Philosophy of History*, p. 65 (p. 55).

THE TIME SPIRIT.

A long time is undoubtedly required by Mind in working out Philosophy. . . . But it must be considered, in regard to the slow progress of the world-spirit, that there is no need for it to hasten: "A thousand years are in Thy sight as one day." It has time enough just because it is outside of time, because it is eternal. . . . The saying that Nature arrives at her ends in the shortest possible way, and that this is right, is a trivial one. The way taken by Mind is indirect, accommodating itself, as it does, to circumstances. Considerations of finite life, such as time, trouble, and cost, have no place here. We ought to feel no disappointment that particular kinds of knowledge cannot yet be attained, or that this or that is still absent. In the history of the world progression is slow.—*History of Philosophy*, vol. i. p. 49 (i. p. 36).

The world-spirit eats away the inward substance, but the appearance, the outward form, still remains; at the end, however, it is an empty shell, the new form breaks forth. In such times this spirit appears as if it —having so far proceeded in its development at a snail's pace, and having even retrograded and become estranged from itself—had suddenly adopted seven-leagued boots.—*History of Philosophy*, vol. iii. p. 240 (iii. p. 158).

THE POWER OF LIFE.

Inward, genuine self-movement, or desire, is nothing else than something in itself, and the want of it, the negative of itself, both being regarded as one and the same. Abstract identity with self is not as yet life, but the fact that the positive in itself is negativity, through which it goes outside itself and brings about changes in itself. Life implies a contradiction within the self, and this living force is just the power to apprehend and maintain the contradiction within itself. . . . . Speculative thought consists alone in thought's maintaining the contradiction, and thereby maintaining itself.—*The Science of Logic*, vol. ii. p. 67.

MAN AND HIS LOT.

We may note, in passing, how important it is for any man to meet everything that befalls him with the spirit of the old proverb which describes each man as the architect of his own fortune. That means that it is only himself, after all, of which the man has the usufruct. The other way would be to lay the blame of whatever we experience upon other men, upon unfavourable circumstances and the like. And this is a fresh example of the language of unfreedom, and at the same time the spring of discontent. If a man saw, on the contrary, that whatever happens to him is only the outcome of himself, and that he only bears his own guilt, he would stand free, and in everything that came upon him would have the consciousness that he suffered no wrong. A man who lives in dispeace with himself and his lot commits much that is perverse and amiss, for no other reason than because of the false opinion that he is wronged by others. No doubt, too, there is a great deal of chance in what befalls us. But the chance has its root in the "natural" man. So long, however, as a man is otherwise conscious that he is free, his harmony of soul and peace of mind will not be destroyed by the disagreeables that befall him. It is their view of necessity, therefore, which is at the root of the content and discontent of men, and which in that way determines their destiny itself.—*The Logic*, p. 297 (p. 271).

THE STATE.

A living connection exists only in an articulated whole, whose parts themselves constitute particular, subordinate spheres. But in order to maintain such a connection, the French abstract views of mere number and degree of capacity must be finally set aside, or, at least, no longer made the chief matter, or obtruded as the sole conditions in one of the most important political functions. Such atomistic principles are, both in science and politics, destructive of all rational conceptions, organisation, and life.—*Miscellanies*, vol. i. p. 241.

The development of the Idea has demonstrated that the spirit, as free and rational, is in itself ethical, that the true Idea is actualised rationality, and that this rationality exists as the State. From this idea it is quite easy to infer that its ethical truth assumes for the thinking consciousness a content, which is worked up into the form of universality, and is realised as law. —*Philosophy of Right* (p. 334) (p. 266).

If the State is to have reality as the ethical self-conscious realisation of spirit, it must be distinguished from the form of authority and faith. But this distinction arises only in so far as the ecclesiastical side is divided in itself into separate churches. Then only is the State seen to be superior to them, bringing into existence the universality of thought as the principle of its form. . . . Only through this division has the State been able to develop its true character, and become a self-conscious, rational, and ethical reality.

The State is real. Its reality consists in its realising the interests of the whole in particular ends. Actuality is always the unity of universality and particularity. .... True reality is necessity. What is real is in itself necessary. Necessity consists in this, that the whole is broken up into the differences contained in the Notion. Then, as so broken up, it furnishes a fast and enduring character, not that of the fossil, but that which in giving itself up always begets itself anew. ... Only to a perception which is void of spirit is the State merely finite.—*Philosophy of Right*, p. 339 (p. 270).

The constitution is rational in so far as the active working divisions of the State are in accord with the nature of the Notion. This occurs when every one of its functions is in itself the totality, in the sense that it effectually contains the other elements.— *Philosophy of Right*, p. 344 (p. 274).

In the State we must have nothing which is not an expression of rationality. The State is the world which the spirit has made for itself.—*Philosophy of Right*, p. 346 (p. 276).

Spirit is real only in what it knows itself to be. The State, which is the nation's spirit, is the law which permeates all its relations, ethical observances, and the consciousness of its individuals. Hence the constitution of a people depends mainly on the kind and character of its self-consciousness.—*Philosophy of Right*, p. 352 (p. 282).

The State if it has no middle class is still at a low stage in its development.—*Philosophy of Right*, p. 386 (p. 305).

A representative must have a character, insight, and will equal to the task of participating in public business. He speaks not in his character as an abstract individual, but as one who seeks to make good his interests in an assembly occupied with the universal. And the electors merely ask for some guarantee that the delegate shall carry out and further this universal.—*Philosophy of Right*, p. 396 (p. 318).

Since the civic community is obliged to support individuals, it has also the right to insist that individuals should care for its subsistence.—*Philosophy of Right*, p. 294 (p. 230).

The individuals of a multitude are spiritual beings, and have a two-fold character. In them is the extreme of the independently conscious and willing individuality, and also the extreme of the universality, which knows and wills what is substantive.—*Philosophy of Right*, p. 320 (p. 253).

By patriotic feeling is frequently understood merely a readiness to submit to exceptional sacrifices or do exceptional acts. But in reality it is the sentiment which arises in ordinary circumstances and ways of life, and is wont to regard the commonweal as its substantive basis and end.—*Philosophy of Right*, p. 322 (p. 255).

The State is an organism, or the development of the Idea into its differences. These different sides are the different functions, affairs, and activities of State by means of which the universal unceasingly produces itself by a necessary process.—*Philosophy of Right*, p. 324 (p. 257).

True bravery consists in a readiness to offer up oneself in the service of the State, so that the individual counts only as one amongst many. Not personal fearlessness, but the taking of one's place in a universal cause, is the valuable feature in it.—*Philosophy of Right*, p. 414 (p. 334).

The true atonement and reconciliation has become objective, and unfolds the State as the image and reality of reason. In the State self-consciousness finds the organic development of its real substantive knowing and will; in religion it finds in the form of ideal essence the feeling and the vision of this its truth; and in scientific knowledge it finds the free thought-out knowledge of the same truth—seeing it to be one and the same in all its mutually completing manifestations, namely, the State, nature, and the ideal world.—*Philosophy of Right*, p. 432 (p. 349).

A State is well constituted and internally powerful when the private interest of its citizens is one with the

A GERMAN PHILOSOPHER.

common interest of the State; when the one finds its gratification and realisation in the other—*Philosophy of History*, p. 31 (p. 25).

Ancient rights and ancient constitutions are great and attractive words, just as it sounds wicked to rob a people of their rights. But whether what is called ancient right and constitution is good or bad cannot depend on its age; even the abolition of human sacrifice, of slavery, of feudal despotism, and of innumerable infamies, were all the abrogation of something which was an ancient right. It has often been repeated that rights cannot be lost, that a hundred years of wrong cannot make a right; and it ought to be added that this is so even if the wrong of a hundred years has been called for a hundred years right, and further that the hundred years' actual and positive right justly goes to pieces if the basis which is the condition of its existence falls away.—*Miscellanies*, vol. i. p. 266.

A government may not rest content with merely demanding that something *should* occur, or with the hope that it *may* occur, or with placing restrictions on certain circumstances which might make it difficult for it to occur: it only deserves the name if its regulations are such that what ought to come to pass, is actually brought to pass.—*Miscellanies*, vol. i. p. 244.

THE CONCEPTION OF LAW.

The understanding thinks it has found a universal Law which expresses universal actuality as such; it has however in truth only discovered the conception of

Law, but with this condition also expressed, that all actuality is in itself conformable to Law. The expression "universal attraction" has thus great importance, in so far as it is directed against the unthinking conception to which everything presents itself in the form of contingency, and to which determinateness has the form of sensuous independence.—*The Phenomenology of Spirit*, p. 111.

NATURE.

It is the essential character of Nature to sacrifice itself, to consume itself, so that the Psyche comes forth out of this burnt-offering, and the Idea rises into its proper element, into its own ethereality. This sacrifice of Nature is its process.—*Philosophy of Religion*, vol. i. p. 106 (i. p. 109).

There is no prospect of returning from the uncultured earnestness and troubled sensibility of the modern views of nature to the joyousness and purity of the Greek modes of regarding it, excepting in one way, and that is by restoring the lost identity through speculation, and once more merging the division in a higher potency; once overstepped, any return to the original condition is forbidden.—*Philosophical Treatises*, p. 309.

Nature should be considered as a system of stages, the one of which necessarily proceeds out of the other, and is the next truth to that from which it follows. But yet it is not the case that the one has been naturally derived from the other; the derivation goes on in the inward Idea which constitutes the ground of nature. The metamorphosis which takes place pertains only to the Notion as such, for its change alone is development. But the Notion in nature is in part an inward operation only, and in part it exists only as a living individual; hence to the latter alone is the existent metamorphosis limited.

There has been, both in the older and the more recent philosophy of nature, a blundering tendency to regard development and the transition of a natural form and sphere into one higher, as an outwardly actual process, which yet, in order to make it clearer, has been relegated to the darkness of the past. It is an externality quite peculiar to Nature to let differentiation go on, and independent existences appear; the dialectic Notion which directs the stages is the inwardness of the same. Thinking consideration must rid itself of such nebulous and really sensuous conceptions as, for instance, that of the so-called development of plants and animals out of water, and, further, the process by which the higher animal organisations issue from the lower.—*Philosophy of Nature*, p. 32.

The Notion gives to all particularity an existence in universal fashion. It is quite an empty conception to represent species as gradually evolving themselves in time; distinctions in time have absolutely no interest for thought. If we had to do with enumeration only, and had just to bring before our minds the succession of living creatures one after the other, as they separated themselves into general classes, whether it was that they ever became more developed, richer in determination and content, thereby showing that they had begun from the lowest, or whether the case was reversed, there would always be a universal interest present. There is a general order, as in the division of nature into the three kingdoms, and it is better than if I were to mix them all up together; for this would have something repulsive to the mind, to the Notion, which yearns after knowledge. But it must not be thought that such a dry succession can be made dynamical, or philosophical, or more intelligible, or however else we may like to put it, if the conception of process is used. The animal nature is the truth of the vegetable, this last of the mineral; the earth is the truth of the solar system. In any system, the most abstract comes first, the truth of every sphere is the last; but it likewise is only the first of a higher stage. The completion of one stage from another is the necessity of the Idea; and the diversity of forms must be regarded as one necessary or determinate. But a land-animal does not, of course, proceed from a water-animal; the latter did not fly into the air, nor did the bird come down again to earth. If men wish to compare the stages in nature it is all very well to remark that this animal has one ventricle and that two; but they may not say that pieces have been added, as though this had actually occurred. And no more must the category of earlier stages be applied to the explanation of later, for this is as formal and tiresome as if we were to say the plant is carboniferous, the animal nitrogenous.—*The Philosophy of Nature*, p. 33.

Here [in the doctrines of Evolution, Emanation, &c.] we find the conception of series, in which natural things, and more especially living things, are arranged. The desire to recognise a necessity in such a progression leads us to try to find a law of succession, a fundamental determination which, inasmuch as it posits diversity, likewise repeats itself in this, and thereby begets a new diversity. But the determination of the Notion is not of a nature to go on increasing continually by means of a new addition similar in form; and the observation of ever the same relationship between all the members. This very circumstance of the conception of a series of stages, and such-like, has been the chief obstacle to the conception of the necessity of forms. If planets, metals, or chemical bodies generally, plants, animals, are in this way placed in successive series, and a law for such series is to be looked for, the endeavour will be found a vain one, because nature does not so place her forms in rank and file, and the Notion distinguishes in accordance with qualitative distinctions, and in so far proceeds alone by bounds. The old saying, or as it is called law, *non datur saltus in natura*, is not applicable to the diremption of the Notion; the continuity of the Notion with itself is entirely of another nature.—*The Philosophy of Nature*, p. 36.

DEATH AND LIFE.

The consideration which allies itself with that of change, is that change, while it implies dissolution, involves at the same time the rise of a new life—that while death is the issue of life, life is also the issue of death. This is a grand conception, one which the Oriental thinkers attained, and which is perhaps the

highest in metaphysics. In the idea of Metempsychosis we find it evolved in its relation to individual existence; but a myth more generally known is that of the Phœnix as a type of the Life of Nature.
. . . . But this image is but an Asiatic image, oriental, not occidental. Spirit, consuming the envelope of its existence, does not merely pass into another envelope, nor rise rejuvenescent from the ashes of its previous form; it comes forth exalted, glorified, a purer spirit. It certainly makes war upon itself—consumes its own existence; but in this very destruction it works up that existence into a new form, and each successive phase becomes in its turn a material, working on which it exalts itself to a new grade. . . . The abstract conception of mere change gives place to the thought of Spirit manifesting, developing, and perfecting its powers in every direction which its manifold nature can follow. . . . . It will often see its endeavours fail; often sink under the complications in which it is entangled either by Nature or itself. But in such cases it perishes in fulfilling its own destiny and proper function.—*Philosophy of History*, p. 90 (p. 76).

DEATH.

That which is limited to a natural life cannot through itself rise above its immediate existence; but it is driven beyond this by another, and this process of thrusting out by force, is its death.—*The Phenomenology of Spirit*, p. 63.

We say that man is mortal, and seem to think that the ground of his death is in external circumstances only; so that if this way of looking at it were correct, man would have two special properties, vitality, and also mortality. But the true view of the matter is that life, as life, involves the germ of death, and that the finite, being radically self-contradictory, involves its own self-suppression.—*The Logic*, p. 152 (p. 148).

The living being dies, because it is a contradiction. Implicitly it is the universal or Kind, and yet immediately it exists as an individual only. Death shows the Kind to be the power that rules the immediate individual. For the animal the process of Kind is the highest point of its vitality. But the animal never gets so far in its Kind as to have a being of its own; it succumbs to the power of Kind. In the process of Kind the immediate living being mediates itself with itself, and thus rises above its immediacy, only, however, to sink back into it again. Life thus runs away, in the first instance, only into the false infinity of the progress *ad infinitum*. The real result, however, of the process of life, in the point of its Notion, is to merge and overcome that immediacy with which the idea, in the shape of life, is still beset.—*The Logic*, p. 395 (p. 361).

LOVE.

Morality, Love, just mean the giving up of all particularity, or of the particular personality, and its extension to universality; and so, too, is it with the family and friendship, for there you have the identity of the one with the other. Inasmuch as I act rightly towards another, I consider him as identical with myself. In friendship and love I give up my abstract personality, and in this way win it back as concrete personality. —*Philosophy of Religion*, vol. ii. p. 239 (iii. p. 24).

If love is to be pure, it must first renounce selfishness, it must have freed itself, and Spirit is only freed when it has come outside of itself, and has once beheld the Substantial as Another and a Higher over against itself. . . . That is to say, the fear of God is the presupposition of true love.—*Philosophy of Religion*, vol. i. p. 145 (i. p. 149).

When we say God is Love, we are expressing a very great and true thought. . . . For love implies a distinguishing between two, and yet these two are, as a matter of fact, not distinguished from one another. Love, this sense of being outside myself, is the feeling and consciousness of this identity. My self-consciousness is not in myself, but in another; but this Other in whom alone I find satisfaction and am at peace with myself—and I exist only in so far as I am at peace with myself, for if I had not this inner peace I would be the contradiction which breaks itself up into parts—this Other, just because it is outside of me, has its self-consciousness only in me.—*Philosophy of Religion*, vol. ii. p. 227 (iii. p. 10).

Love, speaking generally, is the consciousness of the unity of myself with another. I am not separate and isolated, but win my self-consciousness only in renouncing my independent existence, and in knowing myself as unity of myself with another, and of another with me.—*Philosophy of Right*, p. 216 (p. 164).

APPARENT DEPTH.

That which is hidden very easily seems to men deep, or as if depth were concealed beneath—depth as a brook is deep when one cannot see the bottom.—*History of Philosophy*, vol. i. p. 105 (i. p. 89).

The less clear the thoughts, the deeper they appear; the most essential but most difficult thing is to express oneself in definite conceptions, and this is forgotten.—*History of Philosophy*, vol. i. p. 213 (i. p. 195).

YOUTH.

Youth thinks it a joy to escape from the home, and, like Robinson Crusoe, to inhabit a desert island. The mistake of first seeking to find depth in the form of remoteness is a necessary one; the depth and strength which we attain can, however, only be measured by the distance we have fled from the central point in which we first found ourselves sunk, and towards which we once more press.—*Miscellanies*, vol. i. p. 142.

TRUE HUMILITY.

It is a very false idea of Christian humility and modesty to desire through one's own abjectness to attain to excellence : this confession of one's own nothingness is really great self-conceit. To attain to true humility we must not remain in our misery, but raise ourselves above it by laying hold of the Divine.— *History of Philosophy*, vol. iii. p. 529 (iii. p. 454).

DEVELOPMENT.

Man cannot possibly receive anything that is given from without, like the wax that is moulded to a form, for everything is latent in the mind of man, and he only seems to learn it. Certainly everything begins from without, but this is only the beginning; the truth is that this is only an impulse towards the development of spirit. All that has value to men, the eternal, the self-existent, is contained in man himself, and has to develop from himself.—*History of Philosophy*, vol. ii. p. 65 (i. p. 410).

That seed-corn with which the life of the plant begins is only in appearance, in an empirical fashion, what is first; for the seed-corn is likewise a product, a result, is what is last. It is the result of the fully developed life of the tree, and incloses this perfect development of the nature of the tree in itself.— *Philosophy of Religion*, vol. i. p. 131 (i. p. 135).

The bud disappears in the bursting forth of the blossom, and it may be said that the one is contradicted by the other; by the fruit, again, the blossom is declared to be a false existence in the plant, and the fruit is judged to be its truth in the place of the flower. These forms not only distinguish themselves from one another, but likewise displace one another as mutually incompatible. But their transient and changing condition also converts them into moments in an organic unity, in which not alone do they not conflict, but in which one is as necessary as the other, and this very necessity first constitutes the life of the whole. But the refutation of a philosophic system, on the one hand, does not usually regard itself in this way; and, on the other, the apprehending consciousness does not commonly know how to free it from its one-sidedness and to keep it so free, or to recognise, in the form of struggling and opposite manifestations, mutually necessary moments.—*The Phenomenology of Spirit*, p. 4.

The thing is not exhausted in its end, but in the process of its realisation; nor is the result the real whole, for it must be taken along with its process: the end on its own account is the lifeless universal, just as the tendency is the mere impulse which still lacks its actuality, and the naked result is the dead body which the tendency has left behind.—*The Phenomenology of Spirit*, p. 5.

Though the embryo is indeed potentially man, it is not yet man in his actuality; in actuality man is man only as cultured reason, which has made itself into that which implicitly it is. And here we first find the actuality of reason. But this result is itself simple immediacy, for it is the self-conscious freedom which rests in itself, and has not set aside the opposite and allowed it so to remain, but which is reconciled with that opposite.—*The Phenomenology of Spirit*, p. 16.

MORALITY.

In the present, morality is regarded as ready to hand, and the place given to actuality causes it to be regarded as not in harmony with morality. But true moral consciousness is operative; in this lies the actuality of its morality. And in action that place is immediately changed; for action is none other than the actualisation of the inward moral end, none other than the bringing forth of an actuality determined through the end, or through the harmony of the moral end and actuality.—*The Phenomenology of Spirit*, p. 450.

Moral action is not something contingent and limited, for it has pure duty as its essence; this constitutes the one complete end, and action, as the actualisation of the same, is thus, with all other limitations of content, the accomplishment of the whole absolute end.—*The Phenomenology of Spirit*, p. 451.

Morality, like formal right, is an abstraction, whose truth is reached only in ethical observance. Hence ethical observance is the unity of the will in its Notion with the will of the individual or subject. —*Philosophy of Right*, p. 68 (p. 41).

Morality in principle is the liberation of the soul from what is foreign and material, its elevation to the domain of pure reason without any other admixture. This purification of the soul is the condition of Philosophy. The moral and the intellectual relationship of all things is hence once more one and the same; it is the relationship to the pure and clearly universal reason, free from matter, free from interposition or foreign mediation.—*Philosophical Treatises*, p. 310.

CHARACTER.

Character is an essential in conduct, and a man of character is an understanding man, who in that capacity has definite ends in view and undeviatingly pursues them. The man who will do something great must learn, as Goethe says, to limit himself. The man who, on the contrary, would do everything, really would do nothing, and fails.—*The Logic*, p. 148 (p. 144).

THE INFINITE END.

Within the range of the finite we can never see or experience that the End has been really secured. The consummation of the infinite End, therefore, consists merely in removing the illusion which makes it seem yet unaccomplished. The Good, the absolutely good, is eternally accomplishing itself in the world; and the result is that it does not need to wait upon us, but is already by implication, as well as in full actuality, accomplished. This is the illusion under which we live. . . . . Only out of this error does the truth arise. In this fact lies the reconciliation with error and with finitude. Error or other-being, when superseded, is still a necessary dynamic element of truth; for truth can only be where it makes itself its own result.—*The Logic*, p. 384 (p. 351).

HAPPINESS.

The stage of reflection that we reach in happiness stands midway between mere desire and the other extreme, which is that of right as right and duty as duty.

In happiness the individual enjoyment has disappeared; the form of universality is there, but the universal does not yet come forth in independence.—*History of Philosophy*, vol. i. p. 181 (i. p. 162).

DUTY.

What is a right is also a duty, and what is a duty is also a right. For a mode of existence is a right only as a consequence of the free substantial will; and the same content of fact, when referred to the will distinguished as subjective and individual, is a duty.—*Philosophy of Mind*, p. 377 (p. 104).

All the aims of society and the State are the private aims of the individuals. But the set of adjustments by which their duties come back to them as the exercise and enjoyment of right, produces an appearance of diversity; and this diversity is increased by the variety of shapes which value assumes in the course of exchange, though it remains intrinsically the same. Still it holds fundamentally good that he who has no rights has no duties, and *vice versa*.—*Philosophy of Mind*, p. 378 (p. 105).

The contradiction in the moral view of the world solves itself, *i.e.*, the difference which rests at its basis reveals itself as being no difference, and converges in pure negativity; this last is just the self, a simple self, which is likewise pure knowledge, as knowledge of itself as this individual consciousness. . . This self, as pure, self-identical knowledge, is clearly the universal, so that this very knowledge as its own knowledge, as conviction, is duty. Duty is no longer the universal which confronts the self, for it is known to have no value in this separation; it is now the law which exists because of the self, not because of which the self exists. —*The Phenomenology of Spirit*, p. 465.

No action can withdraw itself from the judgment of consciousness, for duty for duty's sake, this pure end, is unreal; it finds its reality in the action of the individuality, and action through this has the side of particularity in it. To the valet there are no heroes, not because such an one is not a hero, but because the valet is the valet; the master is not related to the valet as a hero, but as one who eats, drinks, clothes himself. His dealings with him for the most part have to do with supplying individual necessities, and are concerned with the ordinary affairs of life. Similarly there is for judgment no action in which the side of isolated individuality could not be opposed to the universal side of action, and in which there could not be constituted in opposition to the actors, the valets of morality.— *The Phenomenology of Spirit*, p. 486.

ORIGIN OF EVIL.

The question as to the origin of evil may be put better thus: How does the negative enter into the positive? If God in the creation of the world is supposed to be the absolutely positive, then, let man turn where he will, he cannot in the positive find the negative. The view that God permitted evil to exist, involving a passive relation of God to evil, offers no satisfactory solution of the problem. .... Thought desires a reason and a necessary relation, and insists that the negative and positive spring from the self-same root.—*Philosophy of Right*, p. 181 (p. 135).

BADNESS.

A bad man is an untrue man, a man who does not behave as his Notion or his destiny requires. Nothing, however, can subsist if it be *wholly* devoid of identity between the Notion and reality. Even bad and untrue things have being, in so far as their reality still somehow conforms to their Notion. Whatever is thoroughly bad or contrary to the Notion is for that very reason on the road to ruin. It is by the Notion alone that the things in the world have their subsistence; or, as it is expressed in the language of religious conception, things are what they are only in virtue of the divine and thereby creative thought which dwells within them.—*The Logic*, p. 386 (p. 354).

EVIL.

Evil is nothing but the incompatibility between what is and what ought to be.—*Philosophy of Mind*, p. 364 (p. 94).

If we regard Evil as possessing a fixity of its own, apart and distinct from Good, we are to a certain extent right: there is an opposition between them: nor do those who maintain the apparent and relative character

A GERMAN PHILOSOPHER. 37

of the opposition mean that Evil and Good in the Absolute are one, or, in accordance with the modern phrase, that a thing first becomes evil from our way of looking at it. The error arises when we take Evil as a permanent positive, instead of—what it really is— a negative which, though it would fain assert itself has no real persistence, and is, in fact, only the absolute sham existence of negativity in itself.—*The Logic*, p. 73 (p. 71).

GOOD AND EVIL.

However true it is to say that in accordance with this their Notion good and evil—in so far as they are not good and evil—are the same, it is equally true that they are not the same, but clearly different; for Being-for-self, and also pure knowledge, are in like manner pure negativity, or absolute difference, in themselves. These two propositions first complete the whole, and to the assertion and assurance of the first the assertion of the other must with indomitable pertinacity oppose itself. For because both have equal right, both have equal unright, and their unright consists in taking abstract forms such as the same and not the same, identity and non-identity, to be true, fixed, and actual, and to rest altogether on them. Neither the one nor the other is true, but their movement—the fact that the simple identity is abstraction and consequently absolute difference, but that this last as difference in itself, separated from itself, is thus self-identity. This is the case with the identity of the divine Essence and nature generally, and human nature in particular: the former is nature in so far as it is not Essence; the latter is divine in its Essence. But it is spirit in which both abstract sides are set forth as they are in truth—that is, as abrogated. And this position cannot be expressed by judgment and the unspiritual " is," the copula of the above.—*The Phenomenology of Spirit*, p. 565.

RIGHT.

Not because I find a thing not contradictory is it right, but because it is the right is it right. . . . It is through the right being absolute to me that I am present in moral substance; thus it is the essential reality of self-consciousness; and this indeed is its actuality and present existence, its self and will.— *The Phenomenology of Spirit*, p. 315.

CONSCIENCE.

The content of the utterance of conscience is the self which knows itself as essence. It is this alone to which it gives expression, and this expression is the true actuality of action and the value of action. Consciousness expresses its conviction; it is this conviction in which alone action is duty; it holds good as duty likewise through this fact alone, that the conviction is expressed.—*The Phenomenology of Spirit*, p. 476.

ENJOYMENT.

Striving after happiness, after spiritual enjoyment, and talking of the pleasure of science and art, is

A GERMAN PHILOSOPHER.

dull and insipid, for the matter in question no longer has the form of enjoyment, the whole idea of it is gone. . . . The true attitude is to concern oneself with the matter itself, and not with our enjoyment, that is, not with a constant reflection on a relation borne to oneself as individual, but with the matter as matter and as implicitly universal.—*History of Philosophy*, vol. ii. p. 414 (ii. p. 269).

LANGUAGE.

All voices were raised against that miserable learning of Latin; above all, the feeling grew that a people cannot be regarded as cultured until it can express all the treasures of knowledge in its own tongue, and can freely exercise itself therein, whatever be the matter in discussion. This inwardness with which our speech belongs to us is lacking to such learning as we possess only in a foreign tongue.—*Miscellanies*, vol. i. p. 136.

The wealth of this knowledge is, however, bound up with its language, and only through and in this do we attain to it in all its peculiar excellence. Translations may perhaps give us the substance, but not the form, not the ethereal soul. They resemble artificial roses, which in form, colour, and perhaps even sweetness of scent, may have the appearance of reality, but which do not attain to the loveliness, charm, and tenderness of the living rose. . . . Speech is the musical element, the element of inwardness, which disappear in translation, the delicate fragrance through which the sympathy of soul may be enjoyed, but without which the work of the ancients tastes like Rhine-wine which has lost its bouquet.—*Miscellanies*, vol. i. p. 141.

ONE'S MOTHER-TONGUE.

It is not until a thing is expressed in my mother-tongue that it becomes my possession.—*History of Philosophy*, vol. iii. p. 196 (iii. p. 114).

In speech man is productive: it is the first externality that he gives himself, the simplest form of existence which he reaches in consciousness. What man conceives of he inwardly places before himself as spoken. This first form is broken up and rendered foreign if man is in an alien tongue to express or to conceive what concerns his highest interest. . . . . To have in one's possession the right to speak and think in one's own language really belongs to liberty.—*History of Philosophy*, vol. iii. p. 231 (iii. p. 150).

It is of infinite importance that by Luther's translation of the Bible a popular book has been put into the hands of the people, in which the heart, the spirit, can find itself at home in the very highest, in fact in an infinite way; in Catholic countries there is in this respect a grave want. For Protestant peoples the Bible supplies a means of deliverance from all spiritual slavery.—*Philosophy of Religion*, vol. ii. p. 290 (iii. p. 81).

CULTURE.

True culture is not the vanity of directing so much attention to oneself, and occupying oneself with oneself as an individual, but the self-oblivion that absorbs oneself in the matter in hand and in the universal.—*History of Philosophy*, vol. i. p. 224 (i. p. 205).

In culture it is requisite that men should be acquainted with the universal points of view which belong to a transaction, event, &c., that this point of view, and thereby the thing, should be grasped in a universal way, in order to afford a present knowledge of what is in question. . . . A man of culture thus knows how to say something of everything, to find points of view in all.—*History of Philosophy*, vol. ii. p. 9 (i. p. 356).

Uneducated men thrust their eccentricities upon your notice, and do not act according to the universal qualities of the object. . . . . . . Education refines particularity, and enables it to conduct itself in harmony with the nature of the object.—*Philosophy of Right*, p. 248 (p. 191).

Culture is essentially concerned with Form; the work of Culture is the production of the Form of Universality, which is none other than Thought.—*Philosophy of History*, p. 502 (p. 434).

ERUDITION.

Erudition signifies for the most part acquaintance with a number of useless things, that is to say, with that which has no intrinsic interest or value further than being known.—*History of Philosophy*, vol. i. p. 23 (i. p. 12).

Our learning is a mass of empirical matter, in which the discovery of a new form, a new worm, or other vermin is held to be a point of great importance.—*History of Philosophy*, vol. ii. p. 5 (i. p. 352).

CLASSICAL KNOWLEDGE.

I do not think I am saying too much when I assert that he who has not known the works of the ancients has lived without knowing what beauty is. —*Miscellanies*, vol. i. p. 139.

LEARNING.

Learning is not merely the treasuring up of words in the memory; it is through thinking that the thoughts of others are seized, and this after-thinking is real learning.—*Philosophy of Right*, p. 107 (p. 74).

KNOWLEDGE.

True thought and scientific insight can be obtained only in the work of the Notion. It alone can bring forth the universality of knowledge which is not the common indeterminateness and barrenness of the ordinary human understanding, but cultured and perfected knowledge; nor is it the uncommon universality of those talents which pertain to reason, and which ruin themselves by means of the idleness and conceit of genius; but it is the truth which has grown into its native form, which is capable of being the possession of all self-conscious reason.—*The Phenomenology of Spirit*, p. 54.

By Kant . . Knowledge is represented as an instrument, as a method and means whereby we endeavour to possess ourselves of the truth. Thus before men can make their way to the truth itself, they must know the nature and function of their instrument. They must see whether it is capable of supplying what is demanded of it—of seizing the object; they must know what in the object the alterations it makes are, in order that these alterations may not be mixed up with the determinations of the object itself. This would appear as though men could set forth upon the search for truth with spears and staves. And a further claim is made when it is said that we must know the faculty of knowledge before we can know, for to investigate the faculties of knowledge means to know them. But how are we to know without knowing? how are we to apprehend the truth before the truth? It is impossible to say. It is the old story of the σχολαστικός, who would not go into the water before he could swim.—*History of Philosophy*, vol. iii. p. 504 (iii. p. 428).

The idea that knowledge comes entirely from without is in modern times found in empirical philosophies of quite a rude and abstract kind, which maintain that everything man knows of the Divine comes as a matter of education and custom, and that mind is thus an indeterminate potentiality merely. Carried to an extreme, this is the doctrine of revelation, in which everything is given from without. In the Protestant religion we do not find this rude idea in its abstract form, for the witness of spirit is an essential part of the faith, *i.e.*, faith demands that the individual subjective spirit shall of itself accept and set forth the determination which comes to it in the form of something given from without.—*History of Philosophy*, vol. ii. p. 190 (ii. p. 44).

With Kant the thinking, understanding, and the sensuous are each of them particular, and they are merely united in an external, superficial way, just as a piece of wood and a leg might be bound together by a cord.—*History of Philosophy*, vol. iii. p. 516 (iii. p. 441).

This conscious identity of finite and infinite, the union in consciousness of both worlds, the sensuous and intellectual, the necessary and free, is Knowledge. Reflection, as the capacity pertaining to the finite, and the infinite opposed to it, are brought together in reason, whose infinitude grasps the finite within itself. —*Philosophical Treatises*, p. 176.

TRUE LEARNING.

Learning, regarded as a mere process of reception and matter of memory, is a most imperfect kind of education. On the other hand, for the young the tendency towards individual reflection and reasoning is equally one-sided, and is carefully to be withstood. The disciples of Pythagoras had to keep silence the first four years of study, *i.e.*, they were allowed to have no fancies or thoughts of their own, nor to bring such to light; for the end of all education is to root up these individual imaginations, thoughts, and reflections which youth may have and form, and the disposition by which such may be had. Thought, as much as will, must commence with obedience. But were learning limited to mere receptivity, the effect would be little better than if the facts or propositions were inscribed in water; not any mere reception of knowledge, but the activity with which it is apprehended, and the power of using it again, makes what was knowledge merely, into our own possession.—*Miscellanies*, vol. i. p. 153.

LIFE AND EDUCATION.

To the great principle of living in the spirit of one's people all other circumstances are subordinate.—*History of Philosophy*, vol. i. p. 256 (i. p. 237).

Life in the universal and for the universal demands, not lame and cowardly gentleness, but gentleness combined with a like measure of energy, which is not occupied with itself and its own sins, but with the universal and what is to be done for it.—*History of Philosophy*, vol. ii. p. 240 (ii. p. 94).

Through education subjection is brought about, and with that a capacity for being good.—*History of Philosophy*, vol. iii. p. 94 (iii. p. 10).

Life, the highest form in which the Idea exhibits itself in Nature, is simply something which sacrifices itself, and whose essence is to become Spirit, and this act of sacrifice is the negativity of the Idea as against its existence in this form.—*Philosophy of Religion*, vol. ii. p. 254 (iii. p. 42).

SCIENCE.

"It is certainly not on the finite ground occupied by the exact sciences that we can expect to meet the indwelling presence of the infinite. Lalande was right when he said he had swept the whole heaven with his glass, and seen no god. In the field of physical science, the universal, which is the final result of analysis, is only the indeterminate aggregate of the external finite — in one word, Matter. — *The Logic*, p. 128 (p. 123).

PEDANTRY.

A statesman of experience and culture is one who knows how to steer a middle course, and has practical understanding, *i.e.*, deals with the whole extent of the case before him, and not with one side of it which expresses itself in one maxim only. On the other hand, he, whoever he is, who acts on one maxim, is a pedant, and spoils things for himself and others.— *History of Philosophy*, vol. ii. p. 6 (i. p. 353).

DRESS.

In the matter of dress, time of eating, &c., we follow convention, because it is not worth while exercising our insight and judgment. He is the most prudent who does as others do.—*Philosophy of Right*, p. 252 (p. 195).

LUXURY.

Diogenes' way of life was not independent, but occasioned by his social surroundings. It was itself an ungainly product of luxury. Where luxury is extreme, there also prevail distress and depravity, and cynicism results from an antagonism to over-refinement.— *Philosophy of Right*, p. 254 (p. 196).

Part Second.

THE NATURE OF GOD.

Why should God not reveal Himself to us if we earnestly seek the knowledge of Him? A light loses nothing by another's being kindled therefrom. . . . If the knowledge of God were kept from us in order that we should know the finite only, and not attain to the infinite, God would be a jealous God, or God would become an empty name. Such talk just signifies that we wish to neglect what is higher and divine, seeking after our petty interests and opinions. This humility is sin—the sin against the Holy Ghost.—*History of Philosophy*, vol. ii. p. 219 (ii. p. 73).

God must be conceived of as Spirit, and the element in which we recognise His presence must be spiritual. "God thunders with His thunder," it is said, "and is yet not known." The spiritual man, however, demands something higher than what is merely natural. If God is to be known as Spirit, He must do more than thunder.—*Philosophy of Religion*, vol. ii. p. 256 (iii. p. 44).

In the Christian religion God has revealed Himself, that is, He has given us to understand what He is;

A GERMAN PHILOSOPHER.

so that He is no longer a concealed or secret existence. And this possibility of knowing Him thus afforded us, renders such a knowledge a duty. God wishes no narrow-hearted souls or empty heads for His children, but those whose spirit is of itself indeed poor, but rich in the knowledge of Him, and who regard this knowledge of God as the only valuable possession.—*Philosophy of History*, p. 19 (p. 15).

The germ of the plant or the child is at first only inwardly a plant or a man. But for that reason the plant or the man as germ is something immediate, external, which has not yet given itself the negative relation to itself, a passive existence, delivered over to other-being. Similarly God in His immediate conception is not Spirit; Spirit is not the immediate, that which is opposed to mediation, but that essence which eternally sets forth its immediacy, and which eternally returns into itself. God is hence, in His immediacy, only nature; or nature is the inward God, not actual as Spirit, and hence not true.—*The Science of Logic*, vol. ii. p. 176.

God, as a living God, and still more as Absolute Spirit, is known only in His action. Men have early been taught to know Him in His works. From them alone can the determinations which are called His qualities proceed, just as in them His Being is to be found. Thus the apprehending knowledge of His work, *i.e.*, of Himself, arrives at the conception of God in His Being and His Being in His conception.—*The Science of Logic*, vol. iii. p. 169.

It has been shown that an exclusive knowledge of the world on its own account and without God, would be nothing more or less than to know the untrue without the light of the truth. To know the world can signify nothing else than to know the truth of the world, the truth in what by itself would be untrue; and this truth is God. Likewise it is only he who knows the world that knows God; he who in the supersensuous essence of God does not likewise know the nature and Person of God, knows not the supernatural element in God.—*Miscellanies,* vol. ii. p. 142.

To know what God as Spirit is—to apprehend this accurately and distinctly in thoughts—requires careful and thorough speculation. It includes in its forefront the propositions: God is God only so far as He knows Himself: His self-knowledge is, further, His self-consciousness in man, and man's knowledge *of* God, which proceeds to man's self-knowledge in God.—*Philosophy of Mind,* p. 448 (p. 176).

When the notion of God is apprehended only as that of the abstract or most real Being, God is, as it were, relegated to another world beyond; and to speak of a knowledge of Him would be meaningless. Where there is no definite quality, knowledge is impossible. Mere light is mere darkness.—*The Logic,* p. 76 (p. 74).

If we consider God as the Essence only, and nothing more, we know Him only as the universal and irresistible Power; in other words, as the Lord. Now the fear of the Lord is, doubtless, the beginning—but only the beginning—of wisdom. . . . Another not uncommon assertion is that God, as the Supreme Being, cannot be known. Such is the view taken by modern "enlightenment" and abstract understanding, which is content to say, *Il y a un être suprême*, and there lets the matter rest. To speak thus, and treat God merely as the supreme other-world Being, implies that we look upon the world before us in its immediacy as something permanent and positive, and forget that true Being is just the superseding of all that is immediate. If God be the abstract supersensible Being, outside of whom, therefore, lies all difference and all specific character, He is only a bare name, a mere *caput mortuum* of abstract understanding. The true knowledge of God begins when we know that things, as they immediately are, have no truth.—*The Logic*, p. 226 (p. 210).

God is revealed here as He is; He is there as He is in Himself, He is there as Spirit. God is attainable only in pure speculative knowledge, is only in it and is it alone, for He is Spirit, and this speculative knowledge is the knowledge of revealed religion.—*The Phenomenology of Spirit*, p. 552.

What would it be but Jealousy, if God denied the knowledge of God to consciousness? He would have thus denied all truth to it, for God alone is the truth; whatever else is true, and yet does not appear divine content, is only true in so far as it is founded in Him and is known from Him; the rest of it is temporal phenomenon. The knowledge of God, of truth, alone raises man above the brute, marking him out and granting him happiness, or rather blessing him, as is taught by Plato and Aristotle, as well as by Christianity.—*Miscellanies*, vol. ii. p. 302.

It is true that God is necessity, or, as we may also put it, that He is the absolute Thing: He is, however, no less the absolute Person. That He is the absolute Person, however, is a point which the philosophy of Spinoza never reached; and on that side it falls short of the true notion of God which forms the content of religious consciousness in Christianity. — *The Logic,* p. 301 (p. 274).

No doubt God is the Object, and, indeed, the Object out and out, confronted with which our particular subjective opinions and desires have no truth and no validity. As absolute object, however, God does not therefore take up the position of a dark and hostile power over against subjectivity. He rather involves it as a vital element in Himself. Such also is the meaning of the Christian doctrine, according to which God has willed that all men should be saved, and all attain blessedness. The salvation and blessedness of men are attained when they come to feel themselves at one with God, so that God, on the other hand, ceases to be for them mere object, and in that way an object of fear and terror, as was especially the case with the religious consciousness of the Romans. But God in the Christian religion is also known as Love, because in His Son, who is one with Him, He has revealed Himself to men as a man amongst men, and thereby redeemed them. All of which is only another way of saying that the antithesis of subjective and objective is implicitly overcome, and that it is our affair to participate in this redemption by laying aside our immediate subjectivity (putting off the old Adam), and learning to know God as our true and essential self.—*The Logic*, p. 366 (p. 334).

RELIGION.

The religion of the moral spirit is its elevation above its actuality, the retreat from its truth to the pure knowledge of itself.—*The Phenomenology of Spirit*, p. 510.

The becoming Man of divine Essence, or the fact that it really and immediately has the form of self-consciousness, is the simple content of absolute religion. In it Essence is known as spirit, or to be spirit is its consciousness regarding itself. For spirit is the knowledge of itself in its manifestation, the holding the essence which is movement, to be in its other-being identity with itself. . . . In this religion divine Essence is thus revealed. Its revelation openly consists in this, that what it is, is known. But it is known just because it is known as spirit, as essence which is really self-consciousness. . . . The good, the just, the holy, the creator of heaven and earth, &c., are predicates of a subject—universal moments, which in this point have their standing-ground, and only for the first time are, in the return of consciousness into thought. Because they are known, their ground and reality, the subject itself is not yet revealed, and likewise the determinations of the universal are not this universal itself.—*The Phenomenology of Spirit*, p. 549.

Undoubtedly it is only when religion is made the foundation that the practice of righteousness attains stability, and that the fulfilment of duty is secured. It is in religion that what is deepest in man, the conscience, first feels that it lies under an absolute obligation, and has the certain knowledge of this obligation; therefore the State must rest on religion, for it is in religion that we first have any absolute certainty and security as regards the dispositions of men and the duties they owe to the State.—*Philosophy of Religion*, vol. i. p. 99 (i. p. 102).

Spirit bears witness to Spirit; this witness is the peculiar inner nature of Spirit. In this the weighty idea is involved that religion is not brought into man from the outside, but lies hidden in himself, in his reason, in his freedom, in fact.—*Philosophy of Religion*, vol. i. p. 160 (i. p. 165).

Religion is the knowledge which Spirit has of itself as Spirit.—*Philosophy of Religion*, vol. ii. p. 196 (ii. p. 333).

The talk about the limitations of human thought is futile; to know God is the only end of Religion. The testimony of the Spirit to the content of Religion is itself Religion; it is a testimony that both bears witness, and at the same time is that witness. The

Spirit proves itself, and does so in the proof.—*History of Philosophy*, vol. i. p. 89 (i. p. 73).

The sins of him who lies against the Holy Ghost cannot be forgiven. That lie is the refusal to be a universal, to be holy, that is, to make Christ divided, separated, to make Him only another person, this particular person in Judea; or else to say that He now exists, but only far away in heaven or some such place, and not in present actual form amongst His people.— *History of Philosophy*, vol. i. p. 90 (i. p. 74).

Though Religion in the inflexibility of its abstract authority, as opposed to thought, declares that "the gates of Hell shall not triumph over it," the gates of reason are stronger than the gates of Hell, not to overcome the Church, but to reconcile itself to the Church.—*History of Philosophy*, vol. i. p. 96 (i. p. 80).

All the various peoples feel that it is in the religious consciousness that they possess truth, and they have always regarded religion as constituting their true dignity, and the Sabbath of their lives. Whatever awakens in us doubt and fear, all sorrow, all care, all the limited interests of finite life, we leave behind on the shores of time; and as from the highest peak of a mountain, far away from all definite view of what is earthly, we look down calmly upon all the limitations of the landscape and of the world, so with the spiritual eye, man, lifted out of the hard realities of this actual world, contemplates it as something having only the semblance of existence, which, seen from this pure region bathed in the beams of the spiritual sun, merely reflects back its shades of colour, its varied tints and lights, softened away into eternal rest.—*Philosophy of Religion*, vol. i. p. 5 (i. p. 3).

The religion, the morality of a limited sphere of life—*e.g.*, that of a shepherd or a peasant—in its intensive concentration and limitation to a few perfectly simple relations of life, has infinite worth; the same worth as the religion and morality of extensive knowledge, and of an existence rich in the compass of its relations and actions.—*Philosophy of History*, p. 46 (p. 38).

We observe an essential union between the objective side—the Idea—and the subjective side—the personality that conceives and wills it. . . . Among the forms of this conscious union, Religion occupies the highest place. In it Spirit, rising above the limitations of temporal and secular existence, becomes conscious of the Absolute Spirit, and in this consciousness of the self-existent Being, recovers its individual interest; it lays this aside in Devotion—a state of mind in which it refuses to occupy itself any longer with the limited and particular.—*Philosophy of History*, p. 61 (p. 51).

You must not look for the principle of your religion in the Sensuous, in the grave among the dead, but in the living Spirit among yourselves.—*Philosophy of History*, p. 476 (p. 409).

When our religious consciousness, resting upon the authority of the Church, teaches us that God created the world by His almighty will, that He guides the stars in their courses, and vouchsafes to all His creatures their existence and their well-being, the question, Why? is still left to be answered. Now it is the answer to this question which forms the common task of empirical science and of philosophy. When religion refuses to recognise this problem, or the right to put it, and appeals to the unsearchableness of the decrees of God, it is taking up the same agnostic ground as is taken up by the mere Enlightenment of the understanding. Such an appeal is no better than an arbitrary dogmatism, which contravenes the express command of Christianity, to know God in spirit and in truth, and is prompted by a humility which is not Christian, but born of ostentatious bigotry.—*The Logic*, p. 274 (p. 251).

If Feeling is made the fundamental characteristic of man, he is brought down to the level of the brute; for the peculiarity of a brute is to have feeling as its determination, and to live in conformity with feeling. If religion in a man takes a feeling as its basis, this feeling is in reality nothing more than the feeling of his dependence; and thus the dog would be the best Christian, since he has this feeling most developed in him, and it is pre-eminent in his life. . . . . But the spirit becomes free and has the feeling of its divine freedom in religion; it is only the free spirit that has religion and can have religion; what is subjugated in religion is the natural feeling of the heart, particular subjectivity; what in it is free, and indeed by this means becomes free, is Spirit.—*Miscellanies*, vol. ii. p. 295.

If the philosophical knowledge of religion is conceived of as something to be reached historically only, then we should have to regard the theologians who have brought it to this point as clerks in a mercantile house, who have only to keep an account of the wealth of strangers, who only act for others, without obtaining any property for themselves. They do, indeed, receive salary, but their reward is only to serve, and to register that which is the property of others. Theology of this kind has no longer a place at all in the domain of thought: it has no longer to do with infinite thought in and for itself, but only with it as a finite fact, as opinion, ordinary thought, and so on.—*Philosophy of Religion*, vol. i. p. 42 (i. p. 41).

These antitheses, finite *or* infinite, subject *or* object, are abstract forms, which are out of place in such an absolutely rich, concrete content as religion is. . . . We shall here remark only that such characteristics as finite and infinite, subject and object—and this is what always constitutes the foundation of that very knowing and over-wise talk—are undoubtedly different, but are at the same time inseparable too. We have an example of this in physics, in the north and south pole of the magnet. It is often said "those characteristics are as different as heaven and earth." That is quite correct; they are absolutely different, but, as is already suggested by the figure just mentioned, they are inseparable.— *Philosophy of Religion*, vol. i. p. 56 (i. p. 55).

DIFFERENT RELIGIONS.

The mere collection and elaboration of the external and visible elements cannot satisfy us either. On the contrary, something higher is necessary, namely, to recognise the meaning, the truth, and the connection with truth; in short, to get to know what is *rational* in them. They are human beings who have hit upon such religions, therefore there must be *reason* in them, and amidst all that is accidental in them a higher necessity..... Religions, as they follow upon one another, are determined by means of the Notion. Their nature and succession are not determined from without: on the contrary, they are determined by the nature of Spirit, which has entered into the world to bring itself to consciousness of itself.—*Philosophy of Religion*, vol. i. p. 78 (i. p. 78).

States and Laws are nothing else than Religion manifesting itself in the relations of the actual world. —*Philosophy of History*, p. 502 (p. 434).

There is no religion without one or another of these two perceptions—without the immediate deifying of the finite, or the perception of God in the finite. This opposition is the only one possible in Religion, and hence only Heathendom and Christianity exist. Outside these two there is nothing other than the Absolute common to both. The former immediately beholds the natural in the divine and spiritual prototypes, while the latter looks through nature, as the infinite Body of God, to what is most inward and the Spirit of God.

For both nature is the ground and source of the perception of the infinite.—*Philosophical Treatises*, p. 308.

HISTORIC RELIGION.

It is impossible for us to think of religion as such without historic relationship, and there can be nothing surprising in the matter if men have accustomed themselves to regarding the historic from the point of view of higher conceptions, and to raising themselves from the relationships of empiric necessity which ordinary knowledge recognises therein, to the unconditioned and eternal necessity through which all that is in history, as also all that is actual in the course of nature, is previously determined.—*Philosophic Treatises*, p. 304.

RELIGION AND THE WORLD.

From time immemorial it has been the custom to assume an opposition between Reason and Religion, as also between Religion and the World; but on investigation, this turns out to be only a distinction. Reason is really the positive existence [Wesen] of Spirit; divine as well as human. The distinction between Religion and the World is merely this, that Religion as such, is Reason in the soul and heart— that it is a temple in which Truth and Freedom in God are presented to the conceptive faculty; the State, on the other hand, regulated by the self-same Reason, is a temple of human Freedom, concerned with the perception and volition of a reality whose purport may itself be called Divine.—*Philosophy of History*, p. 407 (p. 348).

It is a common idea in reference to the power of Religion, abstractly considered, over the hearts of men, that if Christian love were universal, private and political life would both be perfect, and the state of mankind would be thoroughly righteous and moral. This may represent a pious wish, but it does not represent the truth; for Religion is something inward, pertaining only to the conscience. To it all the passions and desires are opposed, and in order that the heart, will, intelligence, may become true, they must be thoroughly educated. Right must become Custom, Habit; practical activity must be elevated to rational action; the State must have a rational organisation, and then at length does the will of the individual become a truly righteous one.—*Philosophy of History*, p. 411 (p. 351).

MYSTICISM.

We may give the general name of mysticism to the direction of our regard upon the perception of the infinite in the finite. Nothing proves more strikingly that mysticism is the necessary point of view prescribed by the inmost spirit of Christianity, than that even in the extremest opposite, as, for example, in Protestantism, it once again broke through in new, and in some respects even more dark and obscure forms. If the mystics of Christendom found themselves in opposition to prevailing opinion, and were even regarded as heretics and excommunicated, it was because they transformed faith into an intuition, and wished to pluck too soon the still unripened fruit of the times. . . . Perhaps it was essential for the perfect development of the first aim of Christianity that the crystal-clear mysticism of Catholicism, more and more nearly approaching to poetry, should be forced through the prose of Protestantism, within which mysticism first arose in its most developed form.—*Philosophical Treatises*, p. 305.

Mysticism does not signify the concealment of a secret, or lack of knowledge, but consists in this, that the self knows itself to be one with reality, and this reality is hence revealed. The self alone is revealed to itself, or what is revealed is so only in the immediate certainty of itself. But in this, simple reality has been set forth through worship; it has, as serviceable to it, not only such things as pertain to present existence—that which is seen, felt, smelt, tasted—but it is also the object of desires, and is through actual enjoyment one with the self, and thereby perfectly revealed and open to it. That of which it is said that it is revealed to reason or the heart, is really still secret, for the actual certainty of immediate existence is still lacking, the objective certainty as well as that of enjoyment, which, however, in religion is not only the unthinking immediate, but likewise the pure knowing of the self.—*The Phenomenology of Spirit*, p. 524.

FAITH.

The relationship of an absolute finitude to the true absolute is Faith, in which subjectivity recognises itself, indeed, as finite and nothing before the eternal, but yet so regulates this knowledge that it rescues and maintains itself as an implicit existence outside of the absolute.—*Philosophical Treatises*, p. 95.

This connection or relationship of limitation to the Absolute—in which relationship the opposition is alone in consciousness, while regarding the identity entire unconsciousness reigns—is called Faith. Faith does not express the synthesis of feeling or of sensuous perception; it is a relationship of reflection to the Absolute, which in this relationship, indeed, is reason, and certainly negates itself as a separating and separated power, as it also does its products (as individual consciousness); but which has still maintained the form of separation. The immediate certainty of faith, of which, as the ultimate and highest point of consciousness, so much has been said, is nothing more than identity itself, or reason, which, however, does not know itself, but is accompanied by a consciousness of opposition. But speculation raises to consciousness the identity of which the healthy human understanding is unconscious; or it construes the necessary opposition of the common understanding into conscious identity.—*Philosophical Treatises*, p. 181.

This relation—Faith—as the absolute identity of the content with myself, is the same thing as religious feeling, but with this difference, that it at the same time expresses that absolute objectivity which the content has for me. The Church and the Reformers knew perfectly well what they meant by faith. They did not say that men are saved by feeling, by sensation (αἴσθησις), but by faith; so that in the absolute object I have freedom, which essentially includes the renunciation of my own will and pleasure, and of particular conviction.—*Philosophy of Religion*, vol. i. p. 145 (i. p. 150).

Spirit witnesses only of Spirit, and only finite things are mediated by means of external grounds. The true foundation of Faith is the Spirit, and the witness of the Spirit is inherently living. Verification may at first appear in an external formal manner, but this must drop away. . . . True Faith has no accidental content.—*Philosophy of Religion*, vol. i. p. 213 (i. p. 218).

The non-spiritual, from its very nature, is not a content which can belong to Faith. If God speaks, it is spiritually, for the Spirit reveals itself to Spirit alone.—*Philosophy of Religion*, vol. i. p. 214 (i. p. 220).

The absolute essence of faith is really not abstract essence, which is outside believing consciousness, but it is the spirit of the church, it is the unity of abstract essence and self-consciousness.—*The Phenomenology of Spirit*, p. 401.

Religious faith is told that its assurance rests on certain historic evidences, which, considered as historic evidences, certainly would not afford the degree of certainty respecting their content which newspaper intelligences give us regarding any event. It is told that its assurance further rests on the chance conservation of these testimonies—on the preservation by the means of paper on the one hand, and on the other, through the skill and fidelity of the copy from one paper to another, and finally on the right apprehension of the sense of dead words and letters. But really it does not fall to faith to place its certitude on any such testimonies and contingencies. It is in its certainty a spontaneous relation to its absolute object—a pure knowledge of the same, which does not mingle letters, papers, and transcribers in its consciousness of absolute reality, and which is not brought into touch with absolute reality through any such things.—*The Phenomenology of Spirit*, p. 405.

FAITH AND PHILOSOPHY.

A philosophy without heart and a faith without intellect are abstractions from the true life and being of knowledge and faith. The man whom philosophy leaves cold, and the man whom real faith does not illumine, may be assured that the fault lies in themselves, not in knowledge and faith. The former is still an alien from philosophy, the latter an alien from faith.—*Miscellanies*, vol. ii. p. 144.

THE MEDIATOR.

The self-imposed death of the Mediator is the abrogation of His objectivity or His particular independent existence; this particular independence has become universal self-consciousness. On the other hand, the universal has, through self-consciousness, and the pure or unreal spirit of mere thought, become actual. The death of the Mediator is death, not on its natural side or in its particular independent existence only; there dies not the already dead shell abstracted from true reality alone, but also the abstraction of divine Essence. For, in so far as its death has not yet accomplished the reconciliation, it is a one-sided existence which knows the simple side of thought as essence in opposition to actuality; this extreme of the self has not yet equal value with essence; this the self first finds in Spirit. The death of this conception thus directly contains the death of the abstraction of the divine essence which is not set forth as self. It is the painful recognition of the unhappy consciousness that God Himself is dead.—*The Phenomenology of Spirit*, p. 569.

ATHEISM.

The charge of Atheism is seldom heard in modern times, principally because the facts and the requirements of religion are reduced to a minimum.—*The Logic*, p. 140 (p. 135).

SCEPTICISM.

Scepticism apprehends the rational falsely, and then proceeds to contradict it. Or it gives the infinite the itch in order to be able to scratch it.—*History of Philosophy*, vol. ii. p. 512 (ii. p. 368).

THE HEART.

Let it not be enough to have principles and religion only in the head; they must also be in the heart, in the feeling. What we merely have in the head is in consciousness in a general way; the facts of it are objective—set over against consciousness, so that as it is put in me (my abstract ego) it can also be kept away and apart from me (from my concrete subjectivity). But if put in the feeling, the fact is a mode of my individuality, however crude that individuality be in such a form; it is thus treated as my *very own*. My own is something inseparate from the actual concrete self; and this immediate unity of the soul with its underlying self in all its definite content is just this inseparability which, however, yet falls short of the ego of developed consciousness, and still more of the freedom of rational mind-life.—*Philosophy of Mind*, p. 117 (p. 21).

The distinction of Intelligence from Will is often incorrectly taken to mean that each has a fixed and separate existence of its own, as if volition could be without intelligence, or the activity of intelligence could be without will. The possibility of a culture of the intellect which leaves the heart untouched, as it is said, and of the heart without the intellect—of hearts which in a one-sided way want intellect, and heartless intellects—only proves at most that bad and radically untrue existences occur.—*Philosophy of Mind*, p. 302 (p. 64).

THE BIBLE.

The Bible-saying, "The letter killeth, but the spirit giveth life," must also be assented to; and the spirit signifies none else than the power which dwells within those who apply themselves to the letter in order that they may spiritually apprehend and animate it. This signifies that it is the conceptions which we bring with us which have in the letter to give efficacy to themselves. . . . To elucidate signifies to make clear, and it must be made clear to *me;* this can be done by nothing excepting what was already present in me.— *History of Philosophy,* vol. iii. p. 97 (iii. p. 12).

We find in the Bible a well-known conception, called in an abstract fashion the Fall, and expressed in an outward and mythical shape. This idea is a very profound one, and represents not what is merely a kind of accidental history, but rather the everlasting, necessary history of mankind.—*Philosophy of Religion,* vol. i. p. 269 (i. p. 276).

WITNESS OF THE SPIRIT.

The highest need of the human spirit is Thought— the witness of the Spirit. . . . The witness of the Spirit in its highest form takes the form of Philosophy, according to which the Notion, purely as such, and without the presence of any presupposition, develops the truth out of itself, and we recognise it as developing, and perceive the necessity of the development in and through the development itself.—*Philosophy of Religion,* vol. ii. p. 202 (ii. p. 340).

If God were present only in feeling, then men would be no higher than the beasts. It is true that He does exist for feeling too, but only in the region of appearance or manifestation. Nor does He exist for consciousness of the rationalistic type. Reflection is certainly thought too; but it has at the same time an accidental character, and because of this its content is something chosen at random, and is limited. God thus exists essentially for Thought. . . . . . Spirit exists for the spirit for which it does exist, only in so far as it reveals and differentiates itself, and this is the eternal Idea, thinking Spirit, Spirit in the element of its freedom. In this region God is the self-revealer, just because He is Spirit; but He is not yet present as outward manifestation. That God exists for Spirit is thus an essential principle.—*Philosophy of Religion*, vol. ii. p. 224 (iii. p. 8).

SPIRIT.

—In this long period the Notion of Spirit . . . . is striving to bring spirit to perfection, to make progress itself, and bring about its development from spirit. It goes ever on and on, because spirit alone is progress. Spirit often seems to have forgotten and lost itself, but, inwardly opposed, it is inwardly ever working forward, until, grown strong in itself, it bursts asunder the crust of earth which divided it from the sun, its Notion, so that the earth crumbles away. . . . This work of spirit to know itself, this activity to find itself, is the life of spirit and the spirit itself.—*History of Philosophy*, vol. iii. p. 618 (iii. p. 546).

It is by reason of his being Spirit that man is man, and from man as Spirit proceed all the many developments of the sciences and arts, the interests of political life, and all those conditions which have reference to man's freedom and will. But all these manifold forms of human relations, activities, and pleasures, and all the ways in which these are intertwined; all that has worth and dignity for man, all wherein he seeks his happiness, his glory, and his pride, finds its ultimate centre in religion, in the thought, the consciousness, and the feeling of God.—*Philosophy of Religion*, vol. i. p. 3 (i. p. 2).

Spirit is this pure perception which calls aloud to all consciousness: Be for yourself or explicitly what you are in yourself or implicitly—rational.—*The Phenomenology of Spirit*, p. 393.

Spirit raises itself above this crowd of things contingent, above the merely outward and relative necessity involved in them, above the Infinite, which is a mere negative, and reaches a necessity which does not any longer go beyond itself, but is in-and-for-itself, included within itself, and is determined as complete in itself, while all other determinations are posited by it, and are dependent upon it.—*Philosophy of Religion* (Proofs of the Existence of God), vol. ii. p. 466 (iii. p. 269).

It is the Spirit, the indwelling Idea, which attests Christ's mission, and for those who believed, and for us who are in possession of the Notion in its developed form, this is verification.—*Philosophy of Religion*, vol. ii. p. 321 (iii. p. 113).

It is recorded that in Athens there was a law according to which any man who had a lighted candle and refused to allow another to light his by its means, was to be punished by death. This kind of communication is illustrated even in connection with physical light, since it spreads and imparts itself to some other thing without itself diminishing or losing anything; and still more it is the nature of Spirit itself to remain in possession of what belongs to it, while giving another a share in what it possesses. . . . What is here suggested is that God is not jealous, but, on the contrary, has revealed and is revealing Himself; and we have here the more definite thought that it is not so-called human reason, with its limits, which knows God, but the Spirit of God in Man; it is, to use the speculative expression previously employed, the self-consciousness of God which knows itself in the knowledge of Man.—*Philosophy of Religion* (Proofs of the Existence of God), vol. ii. p. 397 (iii. p. 194).

Spirit is essentially self-manifestation—its nature is *to be for Spirit*. . . . . It has been said that the world, the material universe, must have spectators, and must be for Spirit or mind; how much more, then, must God be for Spirit.—*Philosophy of Religion*, vol. i. p. 47 (i. p. 46).

We do right to speak to a child of its Creator, and in this way the child forms an idea of God as of some Higher Being; this is grasped by the consciousness in early years, but only in a limited manner; and the foundation thus laid is then further extended and broadened. The One Spirit is, in fact, the substantial foundation; this is the spirit of a people as it takes a definite shape in the various periods of the history of the world. . . This spirit is, in fact, the substantial element, and, as it were, the identical element of nature; it is the absolute foundation of faith. It is the standard which determines what is to be regarded as truth. . . . Each individual, as belonging to the spirit of his people, is born in the faith of his fathers, without his fault and without his desert, and the faith of his fathers is a sacred thing to the individual, and is his authority.—*Philosophy of Religion*, vol. i. p. 217 (i. p. 222).

CONVERSION.

The man who is "converted" gives up his one-sidedness; he has extirpated it himself in his will, which was the permanent seat of the deed, the place of its abode; that is, he destroys the act in its root. It is congenial to our way of feeling that tragedies should have conclusions having in them the element of reconciliation.—*Philosophy of Religion*, vol. ii. p. 136 (ii. p. 267).

SALVATION.

All men are called to salvation; that is what is highest in the Christian Religion and highest in a unique degree. Therefore Christ says, "All sins can be forgiven to men except the sin against the Spirit." The violation of absolute truth, of the Idea of that union of the two sides of the infinite antithesis, is in these words declared to be the supreme transgression. People have from time to time given themselves a deal of trouble, and racked their brains, trying to find out what is the sin against the Holy Spirit, and have smoothed down this significant expression in all kinds of ways in order to get entirely rid of it. Everything can be destroyed in the infinite sorrow of love, but this destroying process itself appears only as inner present Spirit. What is devoid of Spirit appears at first to have no sin in it, but to be innocent; but this is just the innocence which is by its very nature judged and condemned.—*Philosophy of Religion*, vol. ii. p. 315 (iii. p. 108).

THE DEATH OF CHRIST.

The Death of Christ does away with the human side of Christ's nature, and it is just in connection with this death that the transition is made into the religious sphere; and here the question comes how this death is to be conceived of. On the one hand, it is a natural death brought about by injustice, hate, and violence; on the other hand, however, believers are already firmly convinced in their hearts and feelings that they are not here concerned with morality, with the thinking and willing of the subject in itself, or as starting from itself, but that the real point of importance is an infinite relation to God, to God as actually present, the certainty of the Kingdom of God, a sense of satisfaction, not in morality, nor even in anything ethical, nor in the conscience, but a sense of satisfaction beyond which there can be

nothing higher, an absolute relation to God Himself.—
Philosophy of Religion, vol. ii. p. 296 (iii. p. 87).

The history of the Atonement . . . is not the history of one individual; on the contrary, it is God who accomplishes what is told in it; *i.e.*, the view which it gives is that this history is the universal and absolute history, the history which is for itself.—*Philosophy of Religion*, vol. ii. p. 304 (iii. p. 95).

CHRIST.

Christ—man as man—in whom the unity of God and man has appeared, has in His death, and His history generally, Himself presented the eternal history of Spirit—a history which every man has to accomplish in himself in order to exist as Spirit, or to become a child of God, a citizen of His Kingdom.—*Philosophy of History*, p. 399 (p. 340).

We do not adopt the right point of view in thinking of Christ as an historical bygone personality merely. So conceived of, the question is asked, What is He unspiritually regarded? Considered only in respect of His talents, character, and morality—as a Teacher and so forth—we place Him in the same category with Socrates and others, though His morality may be ranked higher. But excellence of character, morality, &c.—all this is not the ultimate requirement of Spirit—does not enable man to gain the speculative Idea of Spirit for his conceptive faculty. If Christ is to be looked on only as an excellent, even sinless Being, and nothing more, the conception of the Speculative Idea of Absolute Truth is ignored. But this is what is required, this is the point from which we have to start. Make of Christ what you will exegetically, critically, historically . . . the only real question is, What is the Idea or the Truth in and for itself?—*Philosophy of History*, p. 395 (p. 337).

The real attestation of the Divinity of Christ is the witness of one's own Spirit—not miracles, for only Spirit recognises Spirit.—*Philosophy of History*, p. 396 (p. 338).

CHRISTIANITY.

Comprehended in pure ideality, the antithetic form of Spirit is the Son of God; reduced to limited and particular conceptions, it is the World,—Nature and Finite Spirit. Finite Spirit itself, therefore, is posited as a constituent element in the Divine Being. Man himself is thus comprehended in the Notion of God, and this comprehension may be thus expressed—that the unity of man with God is posited in the Christian religion. But this unity must not be superficially conceived of, as though God were only Man, and Man, without further condition, were God. Man, on the contrary, is God only in so far as he annuls the merely natural and limited in his Spirit, and elevates himself to God. That is to say, it is obligatory on him who is a partaker of the truth, and knows that he himself is an element in the Divine Idea, to give up his merely natural being: for the Natural is the Unspiritual. In the Idea of God, then, is to be found the Reconciliation that heals the pain and inward suffering of man. For suffering is henceforth recognised as an instrument necessary for producing the unity of man with God. This implicit unity exists in the first place only for the thinking speculative consciousness; but it must also exist for the sensuous, representative consciousness—it must become an object for the world, it must appear, and that in the sensuous form of Spirit, which is the human. Christ has appeared—a Man who is God, God who is Man; and thereby peace and reconciliation have accrued to the world.—*Philosophy of History*, p. 394 (p. 336).

Christianity, we know, teaches that God wishes all men to be saved. That teaching declares that subjectivity has an infinite value. And that consoling power of Christianity just lies in the fact that God Himself is known as the absolute subjectivity; so that, inasmuch as subjectivity involves the element of particularity, *our* particular personality, too, is recognised, not merely as something to be solely and simply nullified, but as at the same time something to be preserved.—*The Logic*, p. 296 (p. 270).

The movement of the Notion is, as it were, to be looked upon merely as play; the "other" which it sets up is in reality not an "other." Or, as it is expressed in the teaching of Christianity: not merely has God created a world which confronts Him as an "other"; He has also from all eternity begotten a Son in whom He, a Spirit, is at home with Himself.—*The Logic*, p. 318 (p. 289).

The definition of God, given by what is called Deism, is merely the mode in which the understanding thinks God: whereas Christianity, to which He is known as the Trinity, contains the rational Notion of God.—*The Logic*, p. 348 (p. 317).

The Greek religion is, on the one hand, too much, and, on the other hand, too little anthropomorphic: too much, because immediate qualities, forms, and actions are made divine; too little, because man is not divine as man, but only as a far-away form, and not as "this" and subjective. Man reaches truth because for him it becomes a sure perception that in Christ the λόγος has become Flesh. Thus in the first place we have man attaining to spirituality, and in the second we have man as Christ, in whom this original identity of both natures is known. Now, since man really is this process of being the negation of the immediate, and from this negation attaining to himself—to a knowledge of God—he must consequently renounce his natural will, knowledge, and being. This giving up of natural existence is witnessed in Christ's sufferings and death, and in His resurrection and elevation to the right hand of the Father. . . . In Him this process, this conversion of His other-being into spirit, and the necessity of pain in the renunciation of the natural man, is witnessed; but this pain, the pain of feeling that God Himself is dead, is the starting-point of holiness and of elevation to God.—*History of Philosophy*, vol. iii. p. 88 (iii. p. 4).

The germ of Christianity was the feeling of a division between the world and God; its aim was reconciliation with God, not by raising finitude to infinitude, but by the infinite becoming finite, by God's becoming Man. Christianity set forth this union as the first moment of its manifestation as an object of faith. Faith is the inward certainty which anticipates infinitude.... All symbols of Christianity have the characteristic of representing the identity of God with the world in images. What specially characterises Christianity is the perception of God in the finite.—*Philosophical Treatises*, p. 305.

As all opposites cease to be so, just as each is on its own account absolute within itself, it cannot be doubted that likewise in the path prescribed to Christianity, the other unity, which is the taking of the infinite into the finite, may be made evident in the serenity and beauty of the Greek religion. Christianity as opposition is only the path to perfection: in perfection itself it annuls itself as an opposite. And then heaven has truly come again, and the absolute Evangel has been proclaimed.—*Philosophical Treatises*, p. 307.

It might almost be said that when Christianity is brought back to its first appearing, it is brought down to the level of unspirituality, for Christ Himself says that the Spirit will not come until He Himself has departed.—*History of Philosophy*, vol. iii. p. 98 (iii. p. 14).

On the appearing of Christianity it was said, "My kingdom is not of this world"; but the realisation has and ought to be of the present world. In other words, the laws, customs, constitutions, and all that belongs to the actuality of spiritual consciousness, should be rational.—*History of Philosophy*, vol. iii. p. 106 (iii. p. 21).

Christianity brings God before our intelligence as spirit or mind — not as particularised individual spirit, but as absolute, in spirit and in truth. And for this reason Christianity retires from the sensuousness of imagination into intellectual inwardness, and makes this, not bodily shape, the medium and actual existence of its significance.—*Philosophy of Fine Art*, p. 102 (p. 154).

HISTORICAL CHRISTIANITY.

In the alone sufficing philosophy of Christianity not only does the truth appear in the symbolic garb most worthy of it, but also this symbolism is in so inward a manner the very truth, that the latter can be known to men in no other form of sensuous conception, and this form is to it as essential and eternal as its own self. For it is the historic revelation only which has a personal, living God arbitrarily constituted by no man's reason, one who condescends to take upon Himself a certain form, because only in that way can He be conceivable by us, and yet one who still remains this inconceivable and hence actual God.— *Miscellanies*, vol. i. p. 214.

THE CHURCH.

The activity which we find in the Church as in self-consciousness, which distinguishes itself from its conception, is the bringing forth of that which has become implicit. The dead divine Man, or man-like God, is implicitly universal self-consciousness; He has to become such for this self-consciousness. — *The Phenomenology of Spirit*, p. 566.

From the corruption of the ecclesiastical element—that of the Church—results the higher form of rational thought. Spirit, once more driven back upon itself, produces its work in an intellectual shape, and becomes capable of realising the Rational from the secular principle alone.—*Philosophy of History*, p. 134 (p. 116).

As the individual divine Man has an implicit father but an actual mother, so the universal divine Man, the Church, has its own action and knowledge as its father, but as its mother eternal Love, which it only feels and does not perceive in its consciousness as actual immediate object. Its reconciliation is hence in its heart, but with its consciousness still divided, and its actuality still severed.—*The Phenomenology of Spirit*, p. 572.

This assertion of the Jealousy of God all the more necessarily falls within the sphere of the Christian religion, in that this religion is and will be nothing but the revelation of what God is, and the Christian Church should be nothing but the church into which the Spirit of God is sent, and whose members are led into the knowledge of God by that same Spirit which, because it is Spirit, is not sensuousness and feeling, not a conception of the sensuous, but thought, apprehension, knowledge; and which, because it is the divine, holy Spirit, is none other than the thought and knowledge of God. What would the Christian Church be without this knowledge? What is a theology without the knowledge of God? It is just what a philosophy is without the same—sounding brass and a tinkling cymbal!—*Miscellanies*, vol. ii. p. 302.

PROVIDENCE.

All unsatisfied endeavour ceases when we recognise that the final purpose of the world is accomplished, no less than ever accomplishing itself. Generally speaking, this is the man's point of view; the young imagine that the first thing needful is a thorough transformation. The religious mind, on the contrary, views the world as ruled by Divine Providence, and therefore as correspondent with what it ought to be. But this harmony between the "is" and the "ought to be" is not torpid and rigidly stationary. Good, the final end of the world, has being only while it constantly produces itself. And the world of spirit and the world of nature continue to have this distinction, that the latter moves only in a recurring cycle, while the former certainly makes progress as well.—*The Logic*, p. 407 (p. 373).

THE LETTER OF THE BIBLE.

Luther's translation of the Bible has been of incalculable value to the German people. It has supplied them with a People's Book such as no nation in the

Catholic world can boast of.—*Philosophy of History*, p. 503 (p. 435).

Luther has made the Bible speak German, and you Homer: this is the greatest gift which can be offered to a people; for a people is barbarous and incapable of looking on the best of blessings as its own, when it does not know them in its own language. —Letter to J. D. Voss.—*Miscellanies*, vol. ii. p. 474.

BODY AND SOUL.

In the effort after purification morality and philosophy meet. The road to this liberation is not the merely negative conception of finitude, *i.e.*, that it is a limit placed upon the soul; for in such a way it will not be overcome. A positive conception and a like intuition of the implicit is required; for he who knows that only in appearance is the natural separated from the divine, that the body is only in imperfect knowledge body, and separated from the soul, and that in the implicit it is one with the soul, will most exercise himself in dying that death so praised by Socrates, which is the entrance to eternal freedom and true life.... The true triumph, the ultimate liberation of the soul, rests in absolute idealism alone, in the absolute death of the real as such.—*Philosophical Treatises*, p. 311.

IMMORTALITY.

The immortality of the soul must not be represented as first entering the sphere of reality at a later stage;

A GERMAN PHILOSOPHER. 83

it is the actual present quality of Spirit; Spirit is eternal, and for this reason is already present. . . . Man is immortal in consequence of knowledge, for it is only as a thinking being that he is not a mortal, animal soul, and is a free, pure soul. Reasoned knowledge, thought, is the root of his life, of his immortality as a totality in himself.—*Philosophy of Religion*, vol. ii. p. 268 (iii. p. 57).

RECONCILIATION.

The breaking of the hard heart, and its being raised to universality, is the same movement which was expressed in the consciousness that knew itself. The wounds of the spirit heal without leaving any scars; the deed is not imperishable, but is taken back by spirit within itself, and the side of individuality which is in it, whether there by design or as existent negativity, and limit, is the side which immediately vanishes.—*The Phenomenology of Spirit*, p. 489.

The reconciling " Yes," in which both egos are bereft of their opposing existences, here and now, is the existence of the ego which has extended into the twofold, and which remains therein like itself, and which has in its perfect alienation and opposition the certainty of itself. It is the manifested God in the midst of those who know themselves as pure knowledge.—*The Phenomenology of Spirit*, p. 491.

WORSHIP.

Worship is the eternal process by which the subject posits itself as identical with its essential being.—*Philosophy of Religion*, vol. i. p. 70 (i. p. 70).

Worship is thus finally the presence of the content which constitutes absolute Spirit, and this makes the history of the divine content to be essentially the history of mankind as well—the movement of God toward man, and of man toward God.—*Philosophy of Religion*, vol. i. p. 240 (i. p. 246).

PIETY, FALSE AND TRUE.

It is, indeed, piety of a sort which has reduced the whole organised system of truth to elementary intuition and feeling. But piety of the right kind leaves this obscure region, and comes out into the daylight, where the Idea unfolds and reveals itself. Out of its sanctuary it brings a reverence for the law and truth, which are absolute and exalted above all subjective feeling. . . . Right and ethical principle, the actual world of right and ethical life, are apprehended in thought, and by thought are given rational form, that is, a form of universality and determinateness; and this reasoned right finds expression in law. But feeling which seeks its own pleasure, and conscience which finds right in private conviction, regard the law as their most bitter foe.—*Philosophy of Right,* p. 12 (p. xxii.).

Part Third.

MUSIC.

Music, which concerns itself only with the undefined movement of the inward spiritual nature, and deals with musical sounds as, so to speak, feeling without thought, needs little or no spiritual content to be present in consciousness. It is for this reason that musical talent generally announces itself in very early youth, while the head is still empty, and the heart has been but little moved, and is capable of attaining to a very considerable height in early years, before mind and life have experience of themselves.— *Philosophy of Fine Art*, p. 37 (p. 53).

BEAUTY.

Mind, and mind only, is capable of truth, and comprehends in itself all that is, so that whatever is beautiful can only be really and truly beautiful as partaking in this higher element, and as created thereby. In this sense the beauty of nature reveals itself as but a reflection of the beauty which belongs to mind, as an imperfect, incomplete mode of being, as a mode whose really substantial element is contained in the mind itself.—*Philosophy of Fine Art*, p. 5 (p. 4).

ART.

The Idea as such, although it is the essentially and actually true, is yet the truth only in its generality, and has not taken objective shape; but the Idea as the beautiful in Art is at once the Idea when especially determined as in its essence individual reality, and also an indvidual shape of reality essentially destined to embody and reveal the Idea. This amounts to enunciating the requirement that the Idea and its plastic mould as concrete reality are to be made completely adequate to one another. When reduced to such form, the Idea, as a reality moulded in conformity with the conception of the Idea, is the *Ideal.*— *Philosophy of Fine Art*, p. 94 (p. 141).

The more that works of Art excel in true beauty of presentation, the more profound is the inner truth of their content and thought.—*Philosophy of Fine Art*, p. 95 (p. 142).

The work of Art, since it does not know itself, is essentially incomplete, and (since self-consciousness belongs to the Idea) it needs that completion which it acquires by the relation to it of what is self-conscious. It is in this consciousness that the process takes place by which the work of art ceases to be merely object, and by which self-consciousness posits that which seems to it as an Other, as identical with itself. This is the process which does away with that externality in which truth appears in art, and which annuls these lifeless relations of immediacy; and it is through it that the perceiving subject gives itself the conscious feeling of having in the object *its own* essence.—*Philosophy of Religion*, vol. i. p. 136 (i. p. 140).

Art has the vocation of revealing *the truth* in the form of sensuous artistic shape, of representing the reconciled antithesis just described; and, therefore, has its purpose in itself, in this representation and revelation. For other objects, such as instruction, purification, improvement, pecuniary gain, endeavour after fame and honour, have nothing to do with the work of art as such, and do not determine its conception.—*Philosophy of Fine Art*, p. 72 (p. 105).

The universal need for expression in art, therefore, lies in man's rational impulse to exalt the inner and outer world into a spiritual consciousness for himself, as an object in which he recognises his own self.—*Philosophy of Fine Art*, p. 41 (p. 60).

As a matter of mere imitation, art cannot maintain a rivalry with nature, and if it tries, must look like a worm trying to crawl after an elephant. . . . The fervour of abstract copy is to be likened to the feat of the man who had taught himself to throw lentils through a small opening without missing. He displayed this skill of his before Alexander, and Alexander presented him with a bushel of lentils as a reward for his frivolous and meaningless art.—*Philosophy of Fine Art*, p. 56 (p. 82).

If we continue to speak of an aim or purpose, we must, in the first instance, get rid of the perverse idea which, in asking, "What is the aim?" retains the accessory meaning of the question, "What is the use?" The perverseness of this lies in the point that by it the work of art would be regarded as aspiring to something else, which is set before consciousness as the essential and what ought to be; so that then the work of art would only have value as a useful instrument in the realisation of an end having substantive importance *outside* the sphere of art.—*Philosophy of Fine Art*, p. 72 (p. 105).

In a real work of art the distinguishing feature is that some idea is brought forth—a character is presented in which every trait is determined by this idea; and because this is so, the work of art is on the one hand living, and on the other beautiful, for the highest beauty is just the most perfect carrying out of all sides of the individuality in accordance with the one inward principle.—*History of Philosophy*, vol. ii. p. 48 (i. p. 393).

Art liberates the real import of appearances from the semblance and deception of this bad and fleeting world, and imparts to phenomenal semblances a higher reality born of mind. The appearances of art, therefore, far from being mere semblances, have the higher reality and the more genuine existence, as compared with the realities of common life.—*Philosophy of Fine Art*, p. 12 (p. 15).

By reason of the feeling and insight of which a landscape as depicted by an artist is a manifestation, such a work of mind assumes a higher rank than the mere natural landscape. For everything spiritual is better than anything natural.—*Philosophy of Fine Art*, p. 38 (p. 55).

It is said that nature and its products are a work of God, created by His goodness and wisdom; whereas the work of art is *merely* a human production made after man's devising by man's hands. In this antithesis between natural production as a divine creation and human activity as a merely finite creation, we at once come upon the misconception that God does *not* work in man and through man, but limits the range of His activity to nature alone. This false conception is to be entirely abandoned if we mean to penetrate the true conception of art. Indeed, in opposition to such an idea, we must adhere to the very reverse, believing that God is more honoured by what mind does or makes than by the productions or formations of nature. For not only is there a divinity in man, but in him it is operative under a form that is appropriate to the essence of God, in a mode quite other and higher than in nature. God is a spirit, and it is only in man that the medium through which the divine element passes has the form of conscious spirit that actively realises itself.—*Philosophy of Fine Art*, p. 39 (p. 56).

The universal and absolute need out of which art on its formal side arises, has its source in the fact that man is a thinking consciousness, *i.e.*, that he draws out of himself, and makes explicit for himself, that which he is, and, generally, whatever is.—*Philosophy of Fine Art*, p. 40 (p. 58).

ARCHITECTURE.

It is architecture that pioneers the way for the adequate realisation of the God, and in this its service bestows hard toil upon existing nature, in order to disentangle it from the jungle of finitude and the abortiveness of chance. By this means it levels a space for the God, gives form to His external surroundings, and builds Him His temple as a fit place for concentration of spirit, and for its direction to the mind's absolute objects.—*Philosophy of Fine Art*, p. 106 (p. 161).

Part Fourth.

REASON.

Reason is as cunning as it is powerful. Cunning may be said to lie in the intermediative action which, while it permits the objects to follow their own bent, and act upon one another until they waste away, and does not itself directly interfere in the process, is nevertheless only working out its own aims. With this explanation, Divine Providence may be said to stand to the world and its process in the capacity of absolute cunning. God lets men do as they please with their particular passions and interests; but the result is the accomplishment of, not their plans, but His, and these differ decidedly from the ends primarily sought by those whom He employs.—*The Logic*, p. 382 (p. 350).

Plato knew that there was breaking in upon Greek life a deeper principle which could directly manifest itself only as an unsatisfied longing, and therefore as ruin. Moved by the same longing, Plato had to seek help against it, but had to conceive of the help as coming down from above, and as taking the form of an external special form of ethical observance. He exhausted himself in contriving to stem the course of ruin by means of this new society, but succeeded only in injuring more fatally its deeper motive, the free infinite personality. Yet he has proved himself to be a great mind, because the very principle and central distinguishing feature of his idea is the pivot upon which the world-wide revolution then in process turned:

What is rational is real;
And what is real is rational.

Upon this conviction stand, not Philosophy only, but every unsophisticated consciousness. From it also proceeds the view now under contemplation, that the spiritual universe is the natural. When reflection, feeling, or whatever form the subjective consciousness may assume, regards the present as vanity, and thinks itself to be beyond it and wiser, it finds itself in emptiness, and, as it has actuality only in the present, it is vanity throughout. Against the doctrine that the Idea is a mere idea, figment, or opinion, Philosophy preserves the more profound view that nothing is real excepting the Idea. Hence arises the effort to recognise in the temporal and transient the substance, which is immanent, and the eternal, which is present. The rational is synonymous with the Idea, because in realising itself it passes into external existence. It thus appears in an endless wealth of forms, figures, and phenomena. It wraps its kernel round with a robe of many colours, in which consciousness finds itself at home. Through this varied husk the Notion penetrates in order to touch the pulse, and then finds it throbbing in its external manifestations.—*Philosophy of Right*, p. 16 (p. xxvii.).

To recognise reason as the rose in the cross of the present, and to find delight in it, is a rational insight which implies reconciliation with reality. This reconciliation Philosophy grants to those who have felt the inward demand to conceive clearly, to preserve subjective freedom in substantive reality, and yet, though possessing this freedom, to stand, not upon the particular and contingent, but upon what is self-originated and self-completed.—*Philosophy of Right*, p. 19 (p. xxix.).

Rationality, viewed abstractly, consists in the thorough unity of universality and individuality. Taken concretely, and from the standpoint of the content, it is the unity of objective freedom with subjective freedom, of the general substantive will with the individual consciousness, and the individual will seeking particular ends. From the standpoint of form it consists in action determined by thought-out or universal laws and principles.—*Philosophy of Right*, p. 306 (p. 241).

To him who looks upon the world rationally, the world in its turn presents a rational aspect.— *Philosophy of History*, p. 15 (p. 11).

Reason is spirit, inasmuch as the certainty of being all reality is elevated into truth; and it is conscious of itself as its world, and of the world as itself.— *The Phenomenology of Spirit*, p. 317.

The end of reason, as the universal, all-embracing end, is nothing less than the whole world; an end which proceeds far beyond the content of this individual action, and hence really has to be placed beyond all actual action.—*The Phenomenology of Spirit*, p. 451.

It is hard for man to believe that Reason actually exists; but there is nothing real except Reason; it is absolute Power.—*History of Philosophy*, vol. iii. p. 538 (iii. 464).

Men must openly meet and face their reason, and consider the rationality of right. ... It would seem as though the door were opened for every casual opinion when thought is thus made to supervene upon right. But true thought is not an opinion, but the Notion of the thing itself. The Notion of the thing does not come to us by nature. Every man has fingers, and may have brush and colours, but is not by reason of that a painter. So it is with thought. The thought of right is not a thing which every man has at first hand. True thinking is a thorough knowledge of the object. Hence our knowledge must be scientific.—*Philosophy of Right*, p. 8 (p. xx.).

The only thought which Philosophy brings with it to the contemplation of History is the simple conception of Reason; that Reason is the sovereign of the world; that the history of the world, therefore, presents us with a rational process.—*Philosophy of History*, p. 12 (p. 9).

FALSE REASONING.

Nothing is easier for the "Rationalist" than to point out contradictions in the exposition of the faith, and then to prepare triumphs for its principle of formal identity. If the spirit yields to this finite reflection, which has usurped the title of reason and philosophy ("Rationalism"), it strips religious truth of its infinity, and makes it in reality nought. Religion in that case is completely in the right in guarding herself against such reason and philosophy, and treating them as enemies. But it is another thing when religion sets herself against comprehending reason, and against philosophy in general, and especially against a philosophy of which the doctrine is speculative, and so religious.—*Philosophy of Mind*, p. 454 (p. 182).

An action as concrete contains many essential determinations, any one of which may be given as a reason. The seeking for and giving of reasons, in which "ratiocination" mainly consists, is therefore an endless round, containing no ultimate determination; for each and all one or more good reasons can be given, as also for the opposites of the same, and a number of reasons may be brought forward without any result. . . . . No one of them is the sufficient reason, *i.e.*, the Notion.— *The Science of Logic*, vol. ii. p. 100.

LIBERTY.

The essential, but formally essential feature of mind is Liberty, *i.e.*, it is the Notion's absolute negativity or self-identity. Considered as this formal aspect, it *may* withdraw itself from everything external and from its own externality, its very existence; it can thus submit to infinite *pain*, the negation of its individual immediacy: in other words, it can keep itself affirmative in this negativity and possess its own identity. All this is possible so long as it is considered in its abstract self-contained universality.—*Philosophy of Mind*, p. 24 (p. 6).

No Idea is so generally recognised as indefinite, ambiguous, and open to the greatest misconceptions, as the idea of Liberty, now in common currency with so little appreciation of its meaning. . . When individuals and nations have once got into their heads the abstract concept of full-blown liberty, there is nothing like it in its uncontrollable strength, just because it is the very essence of mind, and that as its very actuality. . . . . . It was through Christianity that this idea came into the world. According to Christianity, the individual *as such* has an infinite value as the object and aim of divine love, destined as mind to live in absolute relationship with God Himself, and have God's mind dwelling in him: *i.e.*, man is implicitly destined to supreme freedom. — *Philosophy of Mind*, p. 374 (p. 100).

FREEDOM.

In a free people reason is in truth actualised; it is the present living spirit in which the individual finds his end—*i.e.*, his universal and individual reality—and this not merely expressed and present in its capacity as some particular thing, seeing that it is itself this reality, and has also already attained its destiny. The wisest men of ancient times have therefore given utterance to the saying that wisdom and virtue consist in living in conformity with the manners and morality of one's people.—*The Phenomenology of Spirit*, p. 258.

When we say of the mind of man that it has freedom, the understanding at once brings up the other quality, which in this case is necessity, saying that if Mind is free it is not in subjection to necessity, and, inversely, if its will and thought are determined through necessity, it is not free—the one is said to exclude the other.... But that which is true, the Mind, is concrete, and its attributes are freedom and necessity. The higher point of view is that Mind is free in its necessity, and finds its freedom in it alone, since its necessity rests on its freedom.—*History of Philosophy*, vol. i. p. 39 (i. p. 26).

The fact that man is in and for himself free, in his essence and as man free-born, was known neither by Plato, Aristotle, Cicero, nor the Roman legislators, even though it is this conception alone which forms the source of law. In Christianity the individual personal mind for the first time becomes of real, infinite value; God wills that all men shall be saved. ... These principles make freedom independent of any such things as birth, standing, and culture. The progress made through them is enormous, but they still come short of this, that to be free constitutes the very idea of man.—*History of Philosophy*, vol. i. p. 63 (i. p. 49).

It is fully fifteen hundred years since, through the influence of Christianity, the freedom of the person began to flourish, and, at least in a small section of the human race, took rank as a universal principle. But the recognition here and there of the principle of the freedom of property is, as it were, a thing of yesterday. This is a good example from world-history of the length of time needed by the spirit to reach self-consciousness, and is a rebuke also to the impatience of opinion.—*Philosophy of Right*, p. 98 (p. 67).

Right concerns Freedom, the worthiest and holiest thing in man, the thing which he must know in so far as it is binding upon him. — *Philosophy of Right*, p. 273 (p. 212).

In thinking about freedom we must not take our departure from individuality or the individual's self-consciousness, but from the essence of self-consciousness. . . . . . The State is the embodiment of concrete freedom. In this concrete freedom personal individuality and its particular interests, as found in the family and civic community, have their complete development. In this concrete freedom, too, the rights of personal individuality receive adequate recognition.— *Philosophy of Right*, p. 313 (p. 246).

The Germanic nations, under the influence of Christianity, were the first to attain the consciousness that man, as man, is free; that it is the freedom of Spirit which constitutes its essence. This consciousness arose first in religion, the inmost region of Spirit; but to introduce the principle into the various relations of the actual world involves a more extensive problem— a problem whose solution and application require a severe and lengthened process of culture. . . . The history of the world is none other than the progress of the consciousness of freedom.—*Philosophy of History*, p. 23 (p. 19).

In the process before us the essential nature of Freedom, which involves in it absolute necessity, is displayed as a coming to consciousness of itself (for it is in its very nature self-consciousness), and thereby realising its existence. Itself is its own object of attainment, and the sole object of Spirit. This result it is, at which the process of the World's History has been continually aiming, and to which the sacrifices that have ever and anon been laid on the vast altar of the earth, through the long lapse of ages, have been offered. This is the only aim that sees itself realised and fulfilled, the only pole of repose amid the ceaseless change of events and conditions, and the sole efficient principle that pervades them. This final aim is God's purpose with the world; but God is the absolutely perfect Being, and can will nothing other than Himself—His own will. The nature of His will —that is, His Nature itself—is what we here call the Idea of Freedom, translating the idea of Religion into that of Thought.—*Philosophy of History*, p. 25 (p. 20).

Man is an end in himself only in virtue of the Divine that is in him—that which was designated at the outset as Reason, and which, in view of its activity and power of self-determination, was called Freedom.—*Philosophy of History*, p. 42 (p. 35).

Freedom, as the *ideal* of that which is original and natural, does not exist as original and natural. Rather must it be first sought out and won, and that by the infinite medial discipline of the intellectual and moral powers.—*Philosophy of History*, p. 51 (p. 42).

Freedom exists in a return into itself alone; the undistinguished is the lifeless; the active, living concrete universal is hence what inwardly distinguishes itself, but yet remains free in so doing.—*History of Philosophy*, vol. ii. p. 213 (ii. p. 67).

Freedom means to be self-contained, or at home with one's self.—*Philosophy of Religion*, vol. i. p. 60 (i. p. 59).

Such nations as do not know that man is free in his own right, live in a condition of torpor, both as regards their form of government and their religion.— *Philosophy of Religion*, vol. i. p. 241 (i. p. 247).

The ordinary man believes that he is free when he is allowed to act capriciously, but precisely in caprice is it inherent that he is not free. When I will the rational, I do not act as a particular individual, but according to the conceptions of ethical observance; in an ethical act I establish, not myself, but the thing. A man who acts perversely exhibits particularity.—*Philosophy of Right*, p. 50 (p. 26).

Freedom characterises rationality; it is what abrogates all limitation in itself. But in community with others it must be given up, in order that the freedom of all who stand in the common bond of rational existence may be possible; and the community is again a condition of freedom. Freedom has to abrogate itself in order to be freedom.—*Philosophical Treatises*, p. 231.

Freedom and necessity are ideal factors, and thus not in real opposition; the absolute can hence not establish itself in either of the two forms as absolute, and the philosophic sciences cannot in the one case be a system of freedom, and in the other a system of necessity.—*Philosophical Treatises*, p. 258.

Man is not free when he is not thinking; for except when thus engaged, he sustains a relation to the world around him as to an other, an alien form of being.— *Philosophy of History*, p. 527 (p. 457).

Freedom and necessity as understood by abstract thinkers are not independently real, as these thinkers suppose, but merely ideal factors (moments) of the true freedom and the true necessity, and to abstract and isolate either conception is to make it false. —*The Logic*, p. 105 (p. 101).

The process of necessity is so directed that it overcomes the rigid externality which it first had, and reveals its inward nature. It then appears that the members, linked to one another, are not really foreign to each other, but only elements of one whole, each of them in its connexion with the other, being, as it were, at home, and combining with itself. In this way necessity is transfigured into freedom—not the freedom that consists in abstract negation, but freedom concrete and positive. From this we may learn what a mistake it is to regard freedom and necessity as mutually exclusive. Necessity, indeed, *quâ* necessity, is far from being freedom; yet freedom presupposes necessity, and contains it as an unsubstantial element in itself. A good man is aware that the tenor of his conduct is essentially obligatory and necessary. But this consciousness is so far from making any abatement from his freedom, that without it real and reasonable freedom could not be distinguished from arbitrary choice—a freedom which has no reality, and is merely potential. A criminal, when punished, may look upon his punishment as a restriction of his freedom. Really the punishment is not foreign constraint to which he is subjected, but the manifestation of his own act; and if he recognises this, he comports himself as a free man. In short, man is most independent when he knows himself to be determined by the absolute idea throughout. It was this phase of mind which Spinoza called *Amor intellectualis Dei.—The Logic*, p. 310 (p. 283).

NECESSITY.

But a close examination of the ancient feeling about destiny, will not by any means reveal a sense of bondage to its power; rather the reverse. This will clearly appear if we remember that the sense of bondage springs from inability to surmount the antithesis, and from looking at what *is*, and what happens, as contradictory to what *ought* to be and happen. In the ancient mind the feeling was more of the following kind: because such a thing is, it is, and as it is, so ought it to be. Here there is no contrast to be seen, and therefore no sense of bondage, no pain, and no sorrow. True, indeed, as already remarked, this attitude towards destiny is void of consolation. But then, on the other hand, it is a frame of mind which does not need consolation, so long as personal subjectivity has not acquired its infinite significance. It is this point on which special stress should be laid in comparing the ancient sentiment with that of the modern and Christian world.—*The Logic*, p. 295 (p. 269).

Necessity is often said to be blind. If that means that in the process of necessity the End and final cause is not explicitly and overtly present, the statement is correct. The process of necessity begins with the existence of scattered circumstances, which appear to have no interconnexion and no concern with one another. These circumstances are an immediate actuality which collapses, and out of this negation a new actuality proceeds. . . . The immediate circumstances fall to the ground as conditions, but are at the same time retained as content of the ultimate reality. From such circumstances and conditions there has, as we say, proceeded quite another thing, and it is for that reason that we call this process of necessity blind. If, on the contrary, we consider teleological action, we have in the end of action a content which is already foreknown. This activity therefore is not blind, but seeing. To say that the world is ruled by Providence implies that design, as what has been absolutely predetermined, is the active principle, so that the issue corresponds to what has been foreknown and forewilled.—*The Logic*, p. 293 (p. 268).

In the simple language of the religious mind, which speaks of God's eternal and immutable decrees, there is implied an express recognition that necessity forms part of the essence of God. In his difference from God, man, with his own private opinion and will, follows the call of caprice and arbitrary humour, and thus often finds his acts turn out something quite different from what he had meant and willed. But God knows what He wills is determined in His eternal will neither by accident from within nor from without; and what He wills He also accomplishes irresistibly.— *The Logic*, p. 294 (p. 269).

Necessity gives a point of view which has important bearings upon our sentiments and behaviour. When we look upon events as necessary, our situation seems at first sight to lack freedom completely. In the creed of the ancients, as we know, necessity figured as

Destiny. The modern point of view, on the contrary, is that of Consolation. And Consolation means that if we renounce our aims and interests, we do so only in prospect of receiving compensation. Destiny, on the contrary, leaves no room for Consolation.—*The Logic*, p. 295 (p. 269).

LIMITATION.

The ideals of youth are limitless in extent; reality is called sad because it does not correspond to that infinite. But active life, efficiency, character, all have this essential condition of fixing themselves upon one definite point; he who wills something great, says the poet, must be able to limit himself.—*Miscellanies*, vol. i. p. 188.

THE DIALECTIC.

The higher dialectic of the Notion does not merely apprehend any phase as a limit and opposite, but produces out of this negative a positive content and result. Only by such a course is there development and true progress. Hence this dialectic is not the outward action of subjective thought, but the personal soul of the content, which unfolds its branches and fruit organically.—*Philosophy of Right*, p. 63 (p. 37).

IDEALISM.

The proposition that the finite is ideal constitutes Idealism. The idealism of philosophy consists in nothing else than the fact of not recognising the finite as a true existent. Every philosophy is really ideal, or, at least, it has the ideal as its principle, and the question is, How far does it carry out this principle? Philosophy is as ideal as religion, for religion does not recognise the finite as true existence, as ultimate and absolute, or as non-posited, uncreated, eternal, and no more does philosophy. The opposition between the idealistic and realistic philosophy is hence without signification.—*The Science of Logic*, vol. i. p. 163.

PHILOSOPHY.

The teaching of Philosophy is precisely what frees man from the endless crowd of finite aims and intentions, by making him so insensible to them, that their existence or non-existence is to him a matter of indifference.—*The Logic*, p. 172 (p. 164).

To refute a philosophy is to exhibit the dialectical movement in its principle, and thus reduce it to a constituent member of a higher concrete form of the Idea.—*The Logic*, p. 177 (p. 168).

The truth of the finite is really its ideality. Similarly, the infinite of understanding, which is co-ordinated with the finite, is itself only one of two finites, no whole truth, but a non-substantial element. The ideality of the finite is the chief maxim of Philosophy; and for that reason every genuine philosophy is Idealism.—*The Logic*, p. 188 (p. 178).

To attach, as do some secret societies of modern times, importance to all sorts of numbers and figures, is to some extent an innocent amusement, but it is also a sign of deficiency of intellectual resource. These numbers, it is said, conceal a profound meaning, and suggest a deal to think about. But the point in Philosophy is not what you may think, but what you do think; and the genuine air of thought is to be sought in thought itself, and not in arbitrarily selected symbols.—*The Logic*, p. 212 (p. 198).

Religion and Philosophy come to be one. Philosophy is itself really worship; it is religion, for in the same way it renounces subjective notions and opinions in order to occupy itself with God. . . . What they have in common is, that they are religion; what distinguishes them from each other is merely the kind and manner of religion we find in each. It is in the peculiar way in which they both occupy themselves with God that the distinction comes out.— *Philosophy of Religion*, vol. i. p. 21 (i. p. 20).

The result of the study of Philosophy is that the walls of separation, which are supposed to divide absolutely, become transparent; and that when we go to the root of things we find that there is absolute accordance, when it was believed there was the greatest opposition.—*Philosophy of Religion*, vol. i. p. 48 (i. p. 47).

This absolute truth, that God is not an abstraction but is concrete, is unfolded by Philosophy, and it is only modern philosophy which has reached the profound thought thus contained in the Notion.— *Philosophy of Religion*, vol. ii. p. 319 (iii. p. 111.).

Philosophy in its concrete Idea is the activity of development in revealing the differences which it contains within itself. .... The concrete alone, as including and supporting the distinctions, is the actual. —*History of Philosophy*, vol. i. p. 47 (i. p. 34).

Every philosophy has been, and still is necessary. None have passed away, but all are affirmatively contained as elements in a whole... No philosophy has ever been refuted. What has been refuted is not the principle of this philosophy, but merely the fact that this principle should be considered final and absolute in character... Our attitude to a philosophy must thus contain an affirmative side and a negative; when we take both of these into consideration, we do justice to a philosophy for the first time. We get to know the affirmative side later both in life and in science; thus we find it easier to refute than to justify.—*History of Philosophy*, vol. i. p. 50 (i. p. 37).

When Philosophy with its abstractions paints grey in grey, the freshness and life of youth has gone; the reconciliation is not a reconciliation in the actual, but in the ideal world.—*History of Philosophy*, vol. i. p. 66 (i. p. 52).

To treat of Philosophy is an idealism, in so far as Thought in its own right is made the principle of Truth.—*History of Philosophy*, vol. i. p. 162 (i. p. 145).

It is one thing to have the Idea of Philosophy, to recognise absolute essence, and quite another to recognise it as the system of the universe, of nature, and of individual self-consciousness, as the whole development of its reality.—*History of Philosophy*, vol. iii. p. 107 (iii. p. 23).

It is, indeed, allowed that a man cannot make shoes unless he is a shoemaker, even although he has the measure, and foot, and also the hands. But when Philosophy is concerned, immediate knowledge signifies that every man as he walks and stands is a philosopher, that he can dogmatize as he chooses, and that he is completely acquainted with Philosophy.—*History of Philosophy*, vol. iii. p. 494 (iii. p. 418).

Philosophy has to consider its object in its necessity, not, indeed, in its subjective necessity or external arrangement, classification, &c.; but it has to unfold and demonstrate the object out of the necessity of its own inner nature.—*Philosophy of Fine Art*, p. 16 (p. 20).

Philosophy awakes in the spirit of governments and nations the wisdom to discern what is essentially and actually right and reasonable in the real world. It was well to call these products of thought, and in a special sense Philosophy, the wisdom of the world; for thought makes the spirit's truth an actual present, leads it into the real world, and thus liberates it in its actuality and in its own self.—*Philosophy of the Mind*, p. 432 (p. 159).

This science must often submit to the slight of hearing even people who have never taken any trouble with it, talking as if they thoroughly understood all about it. With no preparation beyond an ordinary education, they do not hesitate, especially under the influence of religious sentiment, to philosophise and to criticise Philosophy. . . Everybody allows that to make a shoe you must have learned and practised the craft of the shoemaker, though every man has a model in his own foot, and possesses in his hand the natural endowments for the operations required. For Philosophy alone, it seems to be imagined, such study, care, and application are not in the least requisite.—*The Logic*, p. 8 (p. 9).

Philosophy owes its development to the empirical sciences. In return it gives their contents what is so vital to them, the freedom of thought—gives them, in short, an *a priori* character.—*The Logic*, p. 20 (p. 22).

It is by the free act of thought that Philosophy occupies a point of view in which it is for its own self, and thus gives itself an object of its own production. Nor is this all. The very point of view which originally is taken on its own evidence only, must in the course of the science be converted to a result—the ultimate result in which Philosophy returns into itself, and reaches the point with which it began. In this manner Philosophy exhibits the appearance of a circle which closes with itself, and has no beginning as the other sciences have.—*The Logic*, p. 25 (p. 27).

It may be well at the commencement of logic to examine the story which treats of the origin and the bearings of the very knowledge which logic has to discuss. For, though Philosophy must not allow herself to be overawed by religion, or accept the position of existence on sufferance, she cannot afford to neglect these popular conceptions. The tales and allegories of religion, which have enjoyed for thousands of years the veneration of nations, are not to be set aside as antiquated even now.—*The Logic*, p. 55 (p. 54).

Philosophy is knowledge, and it is through knowledge that man first realises his original vocation, to be the image of God. When the record adds that God drove men out of the Garden of Eden to prevent their eating of the tree of life, it only means that on his natural side certainly, man is finite and mortal, but in knowledge infinite.—*The Logic*, p. 57 (p. 56).

It often happens in Philosophy that the half-truth takes its place beside the whole truth, and assumes on its own account the position of something permanent. But the fact is that the half-truth, instead of being a fixed or self-subsistent principle, is a mere element absorbed and included in the whole. The metaphysic of the understanding is dogmatic, because it maintains half-truths in their isolation : whereas the idealism of speculative philosophy carries out the principle of totality, and shows that it can reach beyond the inadequate formularies of abstract thought. . . . Such formularies in their isolation are inadmissible and only come into account as formative elements in a larger Notion. . . . The battle of reason is the struggle to break up the rigidity to which the understanding has reduced everything.—*The Logic*, p. 68 (p. 67).

The most cruel despite is done when everyone is convinced of his ability to pass judgment upon, and discard Philosophy without any special study. No such scorn is heaped upon any other art or science.—*Philosophy of Right*, p. 10 (p. xxi.).

Philosophy, as I have already observed, is an enquiry into the principles of the rational, and therefore an apprehension of the real and present. Hence it cannot be the exposition of a world beyond, which is merely a castle in the air, having no existence excepting in the false conceptions of a one-sided and empty reasoning process.—*Philosophy of Right*, p. 16 (p. xxvi.).

To apprehend what is, is the task of Philosophy, because what is, is the reason. As for the individual, everyone is a son of his time; so Philosophy also is its time apprehended in thoughts. It is just as foolish to fancy that any philosophy can transcend its present world, as that an individual can leap out of his time or jump over Rhodes.—*Philosophy of Right*, p. 18 (p. xxviii.).

Philosophers are the initiated ones, those who have participated in the advance within the innermost sanctuary; others have their particular interests—this dominion, these riches, this girl.—*History of Philosophy*, vol. iii. p. 82 (ii. p. 453).

The great necessity in Philosophy is to possess one living idea; the world is a flower which is eternally produced from one grain of seed.—*History of Philosophy*, vol. iii. p. 557 (iii. p. 483).

The ultimate aim in Philosophy is to reconcile Thought or the Notion with reality. . . The deeper spirit goes within itself, the more vehement is the opposition, the more abundant is the wealth without; the depth is to be measured by the greatness of the craving with which spirit seeks to find itself in what is outside of itself.—*History of Philosophy*, vol. iii. p. 617 (iii. p. 545).

In Philosophy nothing is lost, all principles are preserved, since Philosophy in its final aspect is the totality of forms.—*History of Philosophy*, vol. iii. p. 617 (iii. p. 546).

The foremost requirement of Philosophy is that every thought shall be grasped in its full precision, and nothing allowed to remain vague and indefinite. It is usually added that understanding must not go too far. This is correct in so far as understanding is not an ultimate, but on the contrary finite, and so constituted that when carried to extremes it veers round to its opposite. It is the fashion of youth to dash about in abstractions; but the man who has learnt to know life steers clear of the abstract "either—or," and keeps to the concrete.—*The Logic*, p. 151 (p. 146).

Every Philosophy that deserves the name, embodies the Idea; and, secondly, every system represents one particular factor . . . in the completer principle that follows. Thus the history of Philosophy, in its true meaning, deals not with a past, but with an eternal and veritable present; and, in its results, resembles not a museum of the aberrations of the human intellect, but a Pantheon of Godlike figures. These figures are the various stages of the Idea, as they come forward one after another in dialectical development.—*The Logic*, p. 167 (p. 160).

The true characteristic of a Philosophy is the interesting individuality in which reason has organised a form for itself out of the materials of a particular age; the particular speculative reason finds therein spirit of its spirit, flesh of its flesh: in it it beholds itself as one and the same, as another living existence. Every philosophy is complete in itself, and, like a genuine work of art, has totality within itself.—*Philosophical Treatises*, p. 167.

When the power to unite disappears from the life of mankind, and opposites have lost their living relationship and capacity for change, and attain to independence, the necessity for Philosophy arises. . . In the endless activity of Becoming and producing, reason has united what was separate, and reduced absolute division to a relative position which is conditioned through original identity. When and where, and in what form, such self-reproductions of reason appear as Philosophy, is contingent. This contingency must be apprehended from the fact that the absolute establishes itself as an objective totality.—*Philosophical Treatises*, p. 170.

One word more concerning the desire to teach the world what it ought to be. For such a purpose

Philosophy at least always comes too late. Philosophy, as the thought of the world, does not appear until reality has completed its formative process, and made itself ready. History thus corroborates the teaching of the Notion that only in the maturity of reality does the ideal appear as counterpart of the real, apprehends the real world in its substance, and shapes it into an intellectual kingdom. When Philosophy paints its grey in grey, one form of life has become old, and by means of grey it cannot be rejuvenated, but only known. The owl of Minerva takes its flight only when the shades of night are gathering.—*Philosophy of Right*, p. 20 (p. xxx.).

Philosophy, as occupying itself with the True, has to do with the eternally present. Nothing in the past is lost, for the Idea is ever present; Spirit is immortal; with it there is no past, no future, but an essential now.—*Philosophy of History*, p. 98 (p. 82).

From what has been said, amongst other things it is evident that knowledge is only actual, and capable of being set forth, as Science or as system; further, that a so-called fundamental tenet or principle of Philosophy, if it is true, is for that reason also false, in so far as it is only a fundamental tenet or a principle. Hence it is easy to refute it. The refutation consists in this, that its deficiency is demonstrated; deficient it is, however, because it is only the general or principal, the beginning.—*The Phenomenology of Spirit*, p. 18.

ESSENCE.

We say of a people that the great thing is not what they do or how they behave, but what they are. This is correct, if it means that a man's conduct should be looked at, not in its immediacy, but only as it is explained by his inner self, and as a revelation of that inner self. Still it should be remembered that the only means by which the Essence and the inner self can be verified is their appearance in outward reality; whereas the appeal which men make to the essential life, as distinct from the material facts of conduct, is generally prompted by a desire to assert their own subjectivity, and to elude an absolute and objective judgment.—*The Logic*, p. 227 (p. 210).

DESTINY.

Destiny is merely the manifestation of that which determinate individuality is in itself, in its inward, primeval character of determinateness.—*The Phenomenology of Spirit*, p. 228.

Destiny without the Self is the unconscious night which does not arrive at definiteness, nor attain to the lucidity of self-knowledge.—*The Phenomenology of Spirit*, p. 493.

SELF-CONSCIOUSNESS.

Self-consciousness attains to satisfaction in another self-consciousness alone.—*The Phenomenology of Spirit*, p. 134.

THE SUPERSENSUOUS.

The supersensuous world is a restful kingdom of laws, beyond the world pertaining to perception, it is true, for this last represents law by means of perpetual change alone; but it is likewise present in it, and is its picture, immediate and still.—*The Phenomenology of Spirit*, p. 110.

DOGMATISM.

Dogmatism in the method of thought, both in science and in the study of Philosophy, is none other than the opinion that the truth lies in a proposition which is a permanently established result, or else in one immediately known.—*The Phenomenology of Spirit*, p. 30.

THE IDEA.

Only the infinite, the Idea, is actual. Right exists only as a branch of a whole, or as a vine twining itself about a firmly-rooted tree.—*Philosophy of Right*, p. 204 (p. 154).

Before the pure light of the divine Idea—which is no mere ideal—the phantom of a world whose events are an incoherent concourse of fortuitous circumstances, utterly vanishes. Philosophy wishes to discover the substantial purport, the real side of the divine Idea, and to justify the so-much despised Reality of things; for Reason is the comprehension of the Divine work.—*Philosophy of History*, p. 46 (p. 38).

When we hear the Idea spoken of, we need not imagine something far away beyond this mortal sphere. The Idea is rather what is completely present; and it is found, however confined and degenerated, in every consciousness. We conceive the world to ourselves as a great totality which is created by God, and so created that in it God has manifested Himself to us. We regard the world also as ruled by Divine Providence; implying that the scattered and divided parts of the world are continually brought back, and made conformable to the unity from which they have issued. The purpose of Philosophy has ever been the intellectual ascertainment of the Idea; and everything deserving the name of Philosophy has constantly been based on the consciousness of an absolute unity, where the understanding sees and accepts only separation. It is too late now to ask for proof that the Idea is the truth. The proof of that is contained in the whole deduction and development of thought up to this point. The Idea is the result of this course of dialectic.—*The Logic*, p. 387 (p. 354).

The Idea is the dialectic which for ever divides and distinguishes the self-identical from the differentiated, the subjective from the objective, the finite from the infinite, soul from body. Only on these terms is it an eternal creation, eternal vitality, and eternal spirit. But while it thus passes or rather translates itself into the abstract understanding, it for ever remains reason. The Idea is the dialectic which again makes this mass of understanding and diversity understand its finite nature and the pseudo-independence in its productions, and which brings the diversity back to unity. Since this double movement is not separate or distinct in time, nor indeed in any other way—otherwise it would be only a repetition of the abstract understanding —the Idea is the eternal vision of itself in the other—Notion, which in its objectivity *has* carried out *itself*—object, which is inward design, essential subjectivity.—*The Logic*, p. 389 (p. 356).

The Idea is essentially a process, because its identity is the absolute and free identity of the Notion, only in so far as it is absolute negativity, and for that reason dialectical.—*The Logic*, p. 390 (p. 357).

Further development of the Idea or its further determination is the same thing exactly. Depth seems to signify intensiveness, but in this case the most extensive is also the most intensive. The more intensive is the Mind, the more extensive it is; hence the larger is its embrace.—*History of Philosophy*, vol. i. p. 41 (i. p. 28).

Philosophy is system in development. . . . The progression of the various stages in the advance of Thought may occur with the consciousness of necessity, in which case each in succession deduces itself, and this form and this determination can alone emerge. Or else it may come about without this consciousness, as does a natural and apparently accidental process; so that while inwardly, indeed, the Notion brings about its result consistently, this consistency is not made manifest. This is so in nature;

in the various stages of the development of twigs, leaves, blossoms, and fruit each proceeds for itself, but the inward Idea is the directing and determining force which governs the progression. This is also so with the child, whose bodily powers, and above all whose intellectual activities, make their appearance one after the other simply and naturally, so that those parents who form such an experience for the first time, marvel from whence all that is now showing itself from within, comes.—*History of Philosophy*, vol. i. p. 42 (i. p. 29).

If the Absolute were made up of the finite and the infinite, the abstraction of the finite would undoubtedly be a loss. But in the Idea finite and infinite are one; and hence finitude as such has disappeared, in so far as it is made to have in and for itself truth and reality. However, it is only what in it is negation that has been negated, and thus the true affirmative is set forth.—*Philosophical Treatises*, p. 17.

Because Philosophy in absolute identity recognises neither the one opposite nor the other as existent in its abstraction from the other, and as independent, and since the highest Idea is indifferent to both, and each as considered in its isolation is nothing, it is Idealism.—*Philosophical Treatises*, p. 19.

The dogmatism of the Enlightenment and of Eudæmonism did not consist in making happiness and enjoyment the highest things. For if happiness is grasped as Idea, it ceases to be empirical and contingent, as also sensuous. Rational action and the highest enjoyment are one in the highest existence. And if the highest happiness is the highest Idea, it is a matter of entire indifference whether the highest existence is apprehended from the point of view of its ideality, which, when isolated, becomes rational action, or from the point of view of its reality, which, when isolated, may be termed enjoyment or feeling; for rational action and highest enjoyment, ideality and reality, are both equally in it and identical. No philosophy has any other object than to interpret the highest happiness as Idea.—*Philosophical Treatises*, p. 8.

The absolute Idea is the identity of the theoretic and the practical, each of which, by itself one-sided, contains the Idea, but only as a Beyond which is sought for, and an unattained end. Each is hence a synthesis of endeavour, both having the Idea in itself and not having it, passing from the one thought to the other, yet not bringing the two together, but allowing them to remain in their contradiction. . . . The absolute Idea alone is Being, imperishable Life, self-knowing Truth; and it is all Truth.—*The Science of Logic*, vol. iii. p. 317.

It may indeed be said that in all cases we must commence with the Absolute, as also that all progress is merely its manifestation, in so far as the implicit is the Notion. But because it is first of all implicit only, it is just as really not the Absolute, nor the

Notion as set forth, and likewise not the Idea; for these imply that that implicit Being is merely an abstract, one-sided moment. Progress is hence not a sort of superfluity; it would be such if the commencement were in truth already the Absolute. Progress rather consists in this, that the universal determines itself and is explicitly universal, *i.e.*, just as really individual and subject. In its completion alone is it the Absolute.—*The Science of Logic*, vol. iii. p. 324.

The third stage is the immediate which is such by doing away with mediation, the simple which is simple through-abrogation of difference, the positive through abolishing the negative, the Notion which realises itself through other-Being, and through the abrogation of this reality has come together with itself, and has set forth its absolute reality, its simple relation to self. This result hence is the Truth.—*The Science of Logic*, vol. iii. p. 334.

THE NOTION.

The absolute Notion is the category; it is this, that knowledge and the object of knowledge are the same. Thus what pure perception expresses as different from it, what it calls errors or lies, cannot be other than itself; it can but condemn what it is. What is not rational has no truth, or what is not apprehended does not exist; thus when reason speaks of another than itself, it speaks, in fact, of itself alone; it does not thereby step beyond itself.—*The Phenomenology of Spirit*, p. 399.

The true refutation of an assertion must in reality come to pass in itself, and not through the opposition of other principles which lie outside of it; so infinitely powerful is the nature of the Notion, that in an untrue assertion itself the opposite of the assertion made in it is contained, and often, indeed, expressed. Hence we have only to take such an assertion in itself in order by analysis to demonstrate that opposite, and consequently its inward and unsolved contradiction — *Miscellanies*, vol. ii. p. 139.

LOGIC.

The true business of Logic is to show that the thoughts which as usually employed merely float before consciousness, neither understood nor demonstrated, are really grades in the self-determination of thought. It is by this means that they are understood and demonstrated.—*The Logic*, p. 245 (p. 226).

Forms of thought are first set forth and laid down in the speech of mankind; in our times it cannot be sufficiently often brought to mind that what distinguishes man from the brute is thought. Into everything which is made inward to him, which is brought to his conception, or which he makes his own, speech has forced its way; and what he puts into speech, and sets forth in it, contains, either concealed, intermingled, or developed, a category; this demonstrates how natural Logic is to man, for, indeed, it is his real nature.—*The Science of Logic*, vol. i. p. 10.

Logical reason is the substantial or real, which contains all determinations in itself, and is their solid, absolutely concrete unity.—*The Science of Logic*, vol. i. p. 31.

Logic is thus to be comprehended as the system of pure reason, as the kingdom of pure thought. This kingdom is the truth as it is without concealment, in and for itself. We may put it thus, that this content is the manifestation of God as He is in His eternal essence, before the creation of the natural world and a finite spirit.—*The Science of Logic*, vol. i. p. 33.

The system of Logic is the kingdom of shadows, the world of simple realities, freed from all sensuous concretion. The study of this science, the sojourn and the work in this shadow-kingdom, constitutes absolutely the culture and discipline of consciousness.—*The Science of Logic*, vol. i. p. 44.

ABSOLUTE KNOWLEDGE.

Knowledge is the principle of spiritual life, but it is also, as was remarked, the principle of the healing of the injury caused by disunion.—*Philosophy of Religion*, vol. ii. p. 265 (iii. p. 54).

The true form in which the Truth exists can be the scientific system alone. To help to bring about the result that Philosophy should approach more nearly to the form of science—to the end of being able to set aside its name of love of Knowledge, and to become actual Knowledge itself—this is what I set before me. The inward necessity that knowledge shall be science, rests within its nature, and any explanation of this which is satisfactory, simply is an exposition of Philosophy itself.—*The Phenomenology of Spirit*, p. 6.

The end, absolute Knowledge, or Spirit which knows itself as Spirit, has, as the path which leads to it, the recollection of spirits as they are in themselves, and accomplish the organisation of their kingdom. Their preservation on the side of their free outward existence, as it appears in the form of contingency, is history; but on the side of its organisation, as it is comprehended, the science of manifested knowledge. Both together, history as apprehended, constitute the recollection, and the Golgotha, of absolute Spirit, the actuality, truth, and certainty of its throne, without which it would be a dead solitude only.

From out the bowl of all this spiritual world
Foams up infinitude.

—*The Phenomenology of Spirit*, p. 591.

THE ABSOLUTE.

Common fancy puts the Absolute far away in a world beyond. The Absolute is rather directly before us, so present, that so long as we think, we must, though without express consciousness of it, always carry it with us and always use it.—*The Logic*, p. 50 (p. 50).

The definition which declares the Absolute to be the Idea, is itself absolute. All former definitions come back to this. The Idea is the Truth; for Truth is the correspondence of objectivity with the Notion—not of course the correspondence of external things with my conceptions, for these are only *correct* conceptions held by *me*, the individual person. In the Idea we have nothing to do with the individual, nor with figurate conceptions, nor with external things. And yet, again, everything actual, in so far as it is true, is the Idea, and has its truth by and in virtue of the Idea alone. Every individual being is some one aspect of the Idea; for which, therefore, yet other actualities are needed, which in their turn appear to have a self-subsistence of their own. It is only in them altogether and in their relation that the Notion is realised.—*The Logic*, p. 385 (p. 352).

TRUTH.

The True is the whole. But the whole merely is the essence which accomplishes itself through development. It may be said of the Absolute that it really is result, that only in the end is it what it is in truth; and it is just in this that we find its nature, which is the being actual, subject, or self-development.— *The Phenomenology of Spirit*, p. 15.

The fact that the True is only actual as system, and that substance really is subject, is expressed in the conception which calls the Absolute, Spirit—the most elevated conception, and one which pertains to modern times, and to the religion of these times. The Spiritual alone is the Actual; it is the essence or the implicitly existent, the self-related and determined, the other-being and explicit, and in this determinateness or its manifestation, the self-sufficing and remaining—or it is in and for itself. . . . Spirit, which knows itself so developed as Spirit, is scientific knowledge. It is its actuality and the kingdom which it builds for itself in its own elements.—*The Phenomenology of Spirit*, p. 19.

Truth is eternal; it does not fall within the sphere of the transient, and has no history.—*History of Philosophy*, vol. i. p. 19 (i. p. 8).

If the Truth is abstract it must be untrue.—*History of Philosophy*, vol. i. p. 37 (i. p. 24).

Consciousness as consciousness of the universal is alone consciousness of truth; but consciousness of individuality and action as individual, an originality which becomes a singularity of content or of form, is the untrue and bad. Wickedness and error are thus constituted by isolating thought, and thereby bringing to pass a separation from the universal.—*History of Philosophy*, vol. i. p. 319 (i. p. 296).

Before Truth vanity turns pale; spitefully sneering, it sneaks back into itself. Ask not for a criterion of the truth, but for the Notion of the truth in and for itself; on that fix your gaze.—*History of Philosophy*, vol. iii. p. 582 (iii. p. 509).

The doctrine of Truth consists solely and entirely in its being the doctrine of God, and in its having revealed His nature and work. But the understanding, since it has dissolved all this content, has once more concealed God, and degraded Him to what He was in the time of mere longing after Him, to being the Unknown.—*Miscellanies*, vol. ii. p. 286.

At the present day to know Truth, to know God, is not regarded as man's highest endeavour, and consequently right and duty are unknown.—*Philosophy of Religion*, vol. i. p. 186 (i. p. 191).

In opposition to that kind of truth which wraps itself up in the subjectivity of feeling and imagination, the real truth consists in the tremendous transition of the inner into the outer, of the visions of reason into reality. By this process the whole of world-history has been wrought out, and civilized man has at length won the actuality and the consciousness of a reasonable political life.—*Philosophy of Right*, p. 329 (p. 261).

Truth, with the Lutherans, is not a finished and completed thing; the subject himself must be imbued with Truth, surrendering his particular being in exchange for the substantive Truth, and making that Truth his own. . . . Thus Christian Freedom is actualised.—*Philosophy of History*, p. 502 (p. 433).

ENVY.

Incapable of any great action of its own, envy tries hard to depreciate greatness, and to bring it down to its own level. Let us, rather, recall the fine expression of Goethe, that there is no remedy but Love against great superiorities of others. We may seek to rob men's great actions of their grandness by the insinuation of hypocrisy; but, though it is possible that men in an instance now and then may dissemble and disguise a good deal, they cannot conceal the whole of their inner self, which infallibly betrays itself in the *decursus vitae*. Even here it is true that a man is nothing but the series of his actions.—*The Logic*, p. 279 (p. 255).

MAN'S NATURE.

The primary condition of Man, which is superficially represented as a state of innocence, is the state of nature, the animal state. Man must be culpable; in so far as he is good he must not be good as any natural thing is good, but his guilt, his will, must come into play, it must be possible to impute to him moral acts. Guilt really means the possibility of imputation. The good man is good along with and by means of his will, and to that extent because of his guilt.— *Philosophy of Religion*, vol. ii. p. 260 (iii. p. 48).

So far as man's essential nature is concerned, nothing new is to be introduced into him. To try to do this would be as absurd as to give a dog printed writings to chew, under the idea that in this way you could put mind into it. He who has not extended his spiritual interests beyond the hurry and bustle of this finite world, nor succeeded in lifting himself above this life through aspiration, through the anticipation, through the feeling of the Eternal, and who has not gazed upon the pure ether of the soul, does not possess in himself that element which it is our object here to comprehend. —*Philosophy of Religion*, vol. i. p. 6 (i. p. 4).

This unity of man with God, with nature in the general sense as Potentiality, is undoubtedly the substantial, essential determination. Man is reason, is Spirit; by means of this quality or capacity he is implicitly the True.—*Philosophy of Religion*, vol. i. p. 267 (i. p. 274).

THE FINITE.

The finite is not true, nor is it what it shall be: its existence implies determinateness. But the inward Idea abolishes these finite forms.—*History of Philosophy*, vol. i. p. 50 (i. p. 37).

The true intellectual world is not a Beyond, for the so-called finite is an element in it, and no division exists between this side and that.—*History of Philosophy*, vol. iii. p. 87 (iii. p. 3).

The finite is an essential moment of the infinite in the nature of God, and thus it may be said that it is God Himself who renders Himself finite, who produces determinations within Himself. . . Creation is activity.

In this is involved differentiation, and in this again the moment of the finite, yet this separate existence of the finite must in turn annul itself. For it is God's; it is His Other, and exists notwithstanding in the definite form of the Other of God. It is the Other and the *not* Other; it dissolves or cancels its own self.—*Philosophy of Religion*, vol. i. p. 193 (i. p. 198).

We must rid ourselves completely of this opposition of finite and infinite... The man who does not rid himself of this phantom steeps himself in vanity, for he posits the Divine as something which is powerless to come to itself, while he clings to his own subjectivity, and taking his stand on this, asserts the impotence of his knowledge.... In losing ourselves in the true object itself, we escape from this vanity of the self-maintaining subjectivity, from this Ego, and make serious work with vanity.—*Philosophy of Religion*, vol. i. p. 195 (i. p. 200).

Such a *modesty* of thought as treats the finite as something altogether fixed and *absolute*, is the worst of virtues; and to stick to a post which has no sound ground in itself is the most unsound sort of theory.—*Philosophy of Mind*, p. 36 (p. 9).

KNOWLEDGE.

This is the function of our own and of every age, to grasp the knowledge which is already there, to make it our own, and in so doing to develop it still further, and to raise it to a higher level. In thus appropriating it to ourselves we make it into something different from what it was before.—*History of Philosophy*, vol. i. p. 14 (i. p. 3).

There slumber in the mind of modern times ideas which require for their awakening other surroundings and another present than the abstract, dim, grey thought of olden times.—*History of Philosophy*, vol. i. p. 62 (i. p. 48).

Knowledge brought about the Fall, but it also contains the principle of Redemption.—*History of Philosophy*, vol. ii. p. 104 (i. p. 447).

The Knowledge which is a necessary element in the culture of a people, thus makes its appearance as the Fall from innocence, and as sin. . . But this evil pertaining to thought cannot be prevented by such things as laws; it can and must be the healer of itself through itself alone, if thought is brought to pass through thought itself.—*History of Philosophy*, vol. ii. p. 465 (ii. p. 321).

THE REAL AND IDEAL.

The true ideal is not what *ought* to be real, but what *is* real, and the only real; if an ideal is held to be too good to exist, there must be some fault in the ideal for which reality is too good. . . . For what is real is rational.—*History of Philosophy*, vol. ii. p. 241 (ii. p. 95).

A GERMAN PHILOSOPHER. 133

Nowhere so much as in the case of the soul (and still more of the mind), if we are to understand it, must that feature of "ideality" be kept in view, which represents it as the *negation* of the real, but a negation where the real is put past, virtually retained, although it does not *exist*. The feature is one with which we are familiar in regard to our mental ideas or to memory. Every individual is an infinite treasury of sensations, ideas, acquired lore, thoughts, &c.; and yet the ego is one and uncompounded, a deep, featureless, characterless mine, in which all this is stored up without existing.—*Philosophy of Mind*, p. 149 (p. 25).

Ideality is not something outside of and beside reality: the notion of ideality just lies in its being the truth of reality. That is to say, when reality is explicitly put as what it implicitly is, it is at once seen to be ideality.—*The Logic*, p. 190 (p. 179).

AGE AND EXPERIENCE.

Age generally makes men more tolerant; youth is always discontented. The tolerance of age is the result of the ripeness of a judgment which, not merely as the result of indifference, is satisfied even with what is inferior, but which, more deeply taught by the grave experience of life, has been led to perceive the substantial, solid worth of the object in question. The insight, then, to which—in contradistinction to these ideals—Philosophy is to lead us, is, that the real world is as it ought to be, that the truly good, the universal divine Reason, is not a mere abstraction, but a vital principle capable of realising itself. This Good, this Reason, in its most concrete form, is God.—*Philosophy of History*, p. 45 (p. 37).

PROGRESS.

In actual existence Progress appears as an advancing from the imperfect to the more perfect; but the former must not be understood as *only* the imperfect, but as something which involves the very opposite of itself— the so-called perfect—as a germ or impulse. . . Thus the Imperfect, as involving its opposite, is a contradiction which certainly exists, but which is continually annulled and solved; the instinctive movement—the inherent impulse in the life of the soul—to break through the rind of mere nature, sensuousness, and that which is alien to it, and to attain to the light of consciousness, *i.e.*, to itself.—*Philosophy of History*, p. 70 (p. 59).

THE WILL.

"Who will be great," says Goethe, "must be able to limit himself." By volition alone man enters actuality, however distasteful it may be to him; for indolence will not desert its own self-brooding, in which it clings to a general possibility.—*Philosophy of Right*, p. 48 (p. 24).

The sentence, *In magnis voluisse sat est*, is right, if it means that one should will something great. But he should also carry it out, otherwise his volition is vain. The laurels of mere willing are dry leaves, which have never been green.—*Philosophy of Right*, p. 163 (p. 120).

THE BODY AND SOUL.

The Notion and its existence are two sides, distinct yet united, like soul and body. The body is the same life as the soul, and yet the two can be named independently. A soul without a body would not be a living thing, and *vice versâ*. Thus the visible existence of the Notion is its body, just as the body obeys the soul which produced it. Seeds contain the tree and its whole power, though they are not the tree itself; the tree corresponds accurately to the simple structure of the seed. If the body does not correspond to the soul, it is defective. The unity of visible existence and the Notion, of body and soul, is the Idea. It is not a mere harmony of the two, but their complete interpenetration. There lives nothing which is not in some way Idea.—*Philosophy of Right*, p. 21.

It is only because I in my living body am a free being that my body cannot be used as a beast of burden. In so far as the "I" lives, the soul, which conceives, and, what is more, is free, is not separated from the body. The body is the outward embodiment of freedom, and in it the "I" is sensible. It is an irrational and sophistic doctrine which separates body and soul, calling the soul the thing in itself, and maintaining that it is not touched or hurt when the body is wrongly treated, or when the existence of a person is subject to the power of another.—*Philosophy of Right*, p. 83 (p. 54).

SORROW.

Man is inwardly conscious that in the depths of his being he is a contradiction, and thus there arises an infinite feeling of sorrow in reference to himself. Sorrow is present only where there is opposition to what ought to be, to an affirmative. What is no longer in itself an affirmative has no contradiction, no sorrow in it either; sorrow is just negativity in the affirmative; it means that the affirmative is something self-contradictory, that it is wounded by its own act.—*Philosophy of Religion*, vol. ii. p. 271 (iii. p. 60).

SPIRITUAL BEAUTY.

The Beautiful is essentially the Spiritual making itself known sensuously, presenting itself in sensuous concrete existence, but in such a manner that that existence is wholly and entirely permeated by the Spiritual, so that the sensuous is not independent, but has its meaning solely and exclusively in the Spiritual and through the Spiritual, and exhibits not itself, but the Spiritual.—*Philosophy of Religion*, vol. i. p. 345 (ii. p. 8).

PASSION.

If interest which devotes to an object the whole individuality to the neglect of all other actual or possible interest or claim, with every fibre of volition concentrating all its desires and powers upon it—if this be called Passion, we may affirm absolutely that nothing great in the world has been accomplished without Passion.—*Philosophy of History*, p. 29 (p. 24).

A world-historical individual is not so unwise as to indulge a variety of wishes, to divide his regards. He is devoted to the One Aim, regardless of all else. It is even possible that such a man may treat other great, even sacred interests, inconsiderately; conduct which indeed makes him subject to moral reprehension. But so mighty a form must trample down many an innocent flower—crush to pieces many an object in its path.— *Philosophy of History*, p. 41 (p. 34).

MIND.

The knowledge of Mind is the highest and hardest, just because it is the most "concrete" of sciences. The significance of that "absolute" commandment, *Know thyself*—whether we look at it in itself or under the historical circumstances of its first utterance—is not to promote mere self-knowledge in respect of the *particular* capacities, character, propensities, and foibles of the single self. The knowledge it commands means that of man's genuine reality, of what is essentially and ultimately true and real—of mind as the true and essential being.—*Philosophy of Mind*, p. 3 (p. 3).

The Absolute is Mind (Spirit); this is the supreme definition of the Absolute. To find this definition and to grasp its meaning and burthen, was, we may say, the ultimate purpose of all education and all Philosophy: it was the point to which turned the impulse of all religion and science; and it is this impulse that must explain the history of the world. . . The spirituality of God is the lesson of Christianity.—*Philosophy of Mind*, p. 29 (p. 7).

EQUALITY.

Equality is the abstract identity set up by the mere understanding. . . . Men are equal, it is true, but only as persons, that is, only with reference to the source of possession.—*Philosophy of Right*, p. 84 (p. 55).

EMPIRICISM.

There is a fundamental delusion in all scientific empiricism. It employs the metaphysical categories of matter, force, those of one, many, generality, infinity, &c. Following the clue given by these categories, it proceeds to draw conclusions, and in so doing presupposes and employs the syllogistic form. And all the while it is unaware that it contains metaphysics, in wielding which it makes use of those categories and their combinations in a style utterly thoughtless and uncritical.—*The Logic*, p. 80 (p. 78).

www.ingramcontent.com/pod-product-compliance
Lightning Source LLC
Chambersburg PA
CBHW031501160426
43195CB00010BB/1058